YOUR FACE
IS YOUR FORTUNE
An Introduction To Chinese Face Reading

DR EVELYN LIP

Marshall Cavendish
Editions

© 2009 Marshall Cavendish International (Asia) Private Limited
First published in 1989 by Times Books International as *The Chinese Art of Face Reading*

Illustrations and text © Evelyn Lip
Photographs courtesy of Kenny Lip Yau Sueng

Editors: Gu Jing, Stephanie Pee / Designer: Bernard Go Kwang Meng

Published by Marshall Cavendish Editions
An imprint of Marshall Cavendish International
1 New Industrial Road, Singapore 536196

Other Marshall Cavendish Offices:
Marshall Cavendish Ltd. 5th Foor, 32–38 Saffron Hill, London ECIN 8FH, UK • Marshall Cavendish Corporation. 99 White Plains Road, Tarrytown NY 10591-9001, USA • Marshall Cavendish International (Thailand) Co Ltd. 253 Asoke, 12th Flr, Sukhumvit 21 Road, Klongtoey Nua, Wattana, Bangkok 10110, Thailand • Marshall Cavendish (Malaysia) Sdn Bhd, Times Subang, Lot 46, Subang Hi-Tech Industrial Park, Batu Tiga, 40000 Shah Alam, Selangor Darul Ehsan, Malaysia

Marshall Cavendish is a trademark of Times Publishing Limited

National Library Board Singapore Cataloguing in Publication Data
Lip, Evelyn.
Your face is your fortune : an introduction to Chinese face reading / Evelyn Lip. – Singapore : Marshall Cavendish Editions, c2009.
p. cm.
ISBN-13 : 978-981-261-635-7 (pbk.)
ISBN-10 : 981-261-635-7 (pbk.)

1. Physiognomy. 2. Fortune-telling. 1. Title.

BF851
138 — dc22   OCN268738976

Printed in Singapore by Times Graphics Pte Ltd

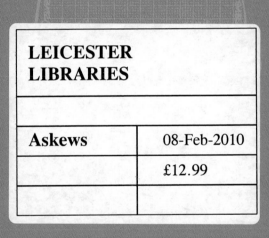

To Kenny & Hua Lin,
Jacqueline & Chee Soon, Francis, Yi Rei & Yi Shaan,
for their.love and support

Contents

Acknowledgements

First and foremost, I wish to express my utmost gratitude to Mr Chris Newson, General Manager for General and Reference publishing of Marshall Cavendish International (Asia) Pte Ltd, for giving me the opportunity to update this book and bring it to the highest level in terms of quality and substance. I'd like to thank my friends and readers who have given me so much encouragement that I have continued to write since 1978. I am grateful for the help given to me in my search for photographs of famous people. Special thanks to Isabel Yeo, librarian, and Alice Tan, researcher, of the Straits Times Library. I also wish to acknowledge my editors, Gu Jing and Stephanie Pee, they are delightful to work with. I am also grateful to the book's designer, Bernard Go.

I wish to thank the Straits Times Press for giving permission to my publisher to publish the photographs in this book. My own illustrations are based on the theory of *ming xiang*. However, many sketches of the famous are based on photographs taken by others. I owe my gratitude to those who have taken these photographs.

I wish to thank my son, Kenny, and my daughter, Jacqueline, for being there for me always. I am also grateful to all those who have in one way or another inspired me to complete this book.

Last but not the least, I wish to acknowledge the lovely photographs taken personally by my son, Kenny Lip Yau Sueng. A special acknowledgement to Ms Margaret Wan for her moral support.

Translation of the Chinese characters (at the top of this page):
Forehead wide, ear lobe round and fleshy, head round, eyebrows well-delineated, eyes clear and refined, chin full, nose tip round like a gall bladder, face square and back fleshy like a tortoise.

A picture is worth a million words and a face a fortune.

半面之交。

This proverb relates the story about a man named Ying Feng who lived in Henan, who wanted to visit his friend. Upon arrival, his friend was not there to receive him. Instead someone opened the door and showed only half his face and then closed the door. Ten years later, Ying Feng was walking on the street and recognised the man who only showed half his face. This illustrates how important the face is in terms of identity.

Preface

My article on *ming xiang* 命相 or face reading was published in 1985 (in the book *Chinese Beliefs and Superstitions*). The encouraging response from my readers prompted me to write and elaborate on this Chinese art of physiognomy that dates as far back as 2000 years ago.

For centuries the Chinese painted the facial features of opera characters with brilliant colours and shades to portray the characters more vividly. They did so because they believed that facial features portrayed the character of a person. There were all kinds of faces: evil, kind, sad, happy, weak, powerful, scholastic, martial, stupid, intelligent and so on. If the character in an opera is sick, the actor will paint a thin red line between the eyebrows, symbolising sickness. For a male general or a heroic male character, the actor would paint an arrow shape in between his eyebrows. This arrow-shaped line starts from between the eyebrows and fades into the forehead. This symbolises the frustrations experienced on the battlefield.

In Chinese history, there were occasions when the face of a person affected his or her fortune. Zhong Kui, a scholar of the Tang dynasty, committed suicide despite topping the imperial examination because the emperor had disqualified him due to his grotesque facial features. Wang Zhao Jun, a great beauty, was not selected to be a concubine because the court artist disfavoured her and painted her image badly.

To the Chinese, the face not only reveals certain personality traits and the spirit of a person, but also his past, present and future. And through the thousands of years of their civilisation, the art of face reading has evolved to ascertain a person's character and fortune. *Ming xiang* or face reading is so important that it is featured every year in the *Tong Shu*, the Chinese Almanac.

This book is an introduction to the art of face reading. It explains the significance of facial features and how they influence a person's wellbeing and fortune, as well as reveal personality traits. There are also detailed studies of facial features of famous people from 551 BC to the present day, comparing their milestones with their facial features. The book also contains many illustrations that will help readers identify the facial features discussed.

The face of Zhong Kui, a scholar of the Tang dynasty, was so grotesque that the emperor disqualified him although he topped the imperial examinations.

The book is also for anyone interested in Chinese culture and beliefs, face reading and metaphysics, and also in the management, observation and assessment of people. However, I wish to say that face reading is not binding for various reasons. There are five factors that govern our wellbeing: *Yi ming, er yun, san feng shui, si daode and wu dushu* 一命，二运，三风水，四道德，五读书. *Ming* 命 implies that a person's fate and destiny is pre-determined by divine powers. *Yun* 运 suggests that a person has good and bad luck during different periods of his or her life. These good and bad times cannot be controlled. Such difficulties impose certain influences on his or her general wellbeing. Feng shui 风水 implies that living or working environments, exert favourable or unfavourable influences on the individual. *Daode* 道德 points out that being virtuous or morally upright improves a person's chances of success. *Dushu* 读书 indicates that family background, upbringing, education and self-improvement also helps a person to improve his or her chances at succeeding. This Chinese phrase means that there are two factors out of human control, namely *ming* and *yun*. So despite having good feng shui, *daode* and *dushu,* we cannot assume 100 per cent success all the time.

This painting shows a young man, a dog and a tree. The dog is looking at its master's face to know what its master wants. The tree is beautiful and magnificent. The tree needs its bark, the way Man needs his face.

Introduction

The theory of *ming xiang* 命相 or face reading is deeply rooted in Chinese culture. Gui Gu Zi who lived during the Warring State Period (481–221 BC) in ancient China wrote a famous book on physiognomy. During the 11th century another book on face reading, called *Mayi Xiang Fa,* was written. These books outline the techniques of face reading. Faces are classified according to the colour, shape and disfigurements of specific areas on the face. Each area refers to a specific age and life situation and by observing the Five Elements of the productive/destructive cycle and the theory of yang and yin, it is possible to make predictions of illnesses or to understand a person's personality.

To the Chinese mind, fate is predestined but one's *yun* 运 (lucky and unlucky spells) can be changed if Man knows the approach of misfortune in advance and searches for ways to avert it in time. On the other hand it may be easier for Man to accept his fate and *yun* or to act positively so that the ill effects may be reduced if he understands the forces at play. Moreover, the Chinese have the philosophy of taking things calmly instead of rashly, going with nature instead of against it, and knowing one's faults instead of ignoring it. Thus the proverb *zhi zi zhi ming* 自知之明, which means that it is advantageous to know one's own virtues and vices, fate and fortune.

Although Man is cannot control destiny, he is still better off knowing the odds, rather than being completely ignorant. *Mian xiang* allows him to find out not only about

Ren yao lian, shu yao pi, which literally translates to 'a person needs a face; a tree needs bark.' Meaning that a person values his reputation just like a trees needs its bark.

himself but also of those around him. Knowing the facial features of family members, business associates, friends and even foes means gaining insight into their personality traits and intellectual capacity. This will help him relate to them better. After all, understanding human nature is essential to any social relationship.

The art of face reading was not exclusive to the Chinese. Western scholars, such as Homer (approx 850 BC) and Hippocrates, also wrote about face reading. By the 18th and 19th centuries, face reading was used in Europe as an aid to the study of criminology. During the 21st century, face reading was sometimes used as a tool in psychoanalysis.

Today, the Chinese art of face reading is still used for analysing a person's intellect, personality and fortune. A physical-emotional profile of the individual can be built up by incorporating the energies of the features. A face reveals the past, present and future. Like in feng shui, face reading is based on the workings of the Five Elements and the balance of yin and yang. According to Chinese beliefs, yin and yang are complementary forces that underpin all things in existence. Facial features can be classified as either yin or yang. Protrusions on the face are yang, while intrusions are yin. Balance (of yin and yang) and proportion are important considerations in face reading. The bone structure is yang while the flesh is yin. The Five Elements (Wood, Fire, Earth, Gold and Fire) can be used to describe the face shape. The harmony and balance of the Elements of facial features is important. Different parts of a face indicate different times of an individual's life. The features on the face are related to the internal organs of the body and can be classified under the Five Elements as shown in Chart 1 below. This is further discussed on pages 43–45.

In Chinese face reading, it is not enough to examine facial features to determine their beauty or wholesomeness. It is also necessary to gauge the compatiability of facial features with their Element (refer to Chart 1).

The Five Elements were conceived as the five forces of nature by the Chinese around the 4th century BC, and these Elements may be positioned in an order of destruction or harmony. The sequence of harmony is Gold, Water, Wood, Fire and Earth. Water is compatible with Wood, Wood with Fire, Fire with Earth, Earth with Gold and Gold with Water. The sequence of destruction is Gold, Wood, Earth, Water and Fire—Earth opposes Water, Water opposes Fire, Fire opposes Gold, Gold opposes Wood and Wood opposes Earth. For example if one's ears are long, fleshy and well-shaped, but the eyes are not perfectly well-formed, the fortune of the person as influenced by the eyes may still be good. This is because the eyes are of Wood Element and compatible with the ears (Water Element). On the other hand if the ears are well-formed but the facial feature of the opposing Element, the eyebrows, are not, the ears cannot influence the fortune of the person depicted by the eyebrows.

Chart 1: Features on the Face and its Corresponding Internal Organs of the Body and Elements

Facial Features	Internal Organs	Elements
forehead	kidneys	Fire
nose	lungs	Gold
mouth / lips	spleen	Earth
ears	kidneys	Water
eyes	liver	Wood
eyebrows	kidneys	Fire

Note: Deformed facial features may be indicative of defects in corresponding internal organs.

However, the art of face reading is not based on theories alone, but also on years of observations by the face reading masters of old. Chinese face readers also believe that the personality of a person is noticeably shown on the face. If a man is confident, his eyes will be bright and he will look you in the eye. If he is nervous, he may stammer and perhaps look sideways. Courage, frankness, industry, cowardice, deception and laziness can all be detected by a close examination of the face and head. Even compassion can be revealed by one's countenance.

Physical behaviour reflects the mental state. Emotional reactions are expressed through the face and body. Therefore past experiences, emotions and expressions mould facial features. Traumatic and sad experiences in life can leave permanent marks on the face just as physical injuries leave behind scars.

As a person matures, physical changes occur not only in the body, but also in the facial features. The biological maturation goes hand in hand with the psychological and physical development including facial maturation. Problems, challenges, anxieties, dissatisfaction, boredom, excitement, enjoyment, hardships, joy and happiness are all registered on the face and these experiences also change facial features. Therefore a face reader can actually read a face and tell the past. A good face reader can even forecast the future based on the features and shape of the face.

The Chinese face reader assesses a person's character and fortune in terms of how balanced the features are in relation to the shape of the face. For example, if a person's head is pointed and face thin and small, he or she may be unsociable and timid and may even encounter bad luck. If one's cheek bones are high but the nose is flat, the personality traits may be that of ill discipline and boastfulness. If the eyes are small in comparison to the overall face, the personality traits may be distrustfulness and dishonesty. If the mouth is small in comparison to the face, the person may be harsh and mean; he may even live a short life. If the cheek bones are too broad the person may be heartless.

Determining personality and predicting behaviour through face reading is most effective by examining sensory receptors such as the eyes, ears, mouth and nose. Vision is the most important sense because it informs the brain about the physical environment resulting in some form of behaviour on the part of the recipient. Eye contact is a very important facial gesture through which behavioural and emotional states can be assessed. Indeed, the eyes are the windows of the mind and soul.

Figures 1, 2 and 3 (page 20) summarises the fortunes of a person at different ages as revealed by different facial features. The age refers to the age of a person according to the Chinese lunar calendar. The Chinese believe that the moment a child is born, he or she is already one year old. Also, a person is a year older not on one's birthday, but on the first day of the lunar new year. For example, if a person is born on the eve of the lunar new year, he is one year old, and the following day, he

Dr. Sun Yatsen's eyes depict his compassion for his countrymen.

is two years old. Generally, to get one's age according to the Chinese lunar calendar, a year is added to the age of the person in that year (ie, according to the solar calendar). Figure 1 identifies various parts of the face, complete with names (the names are applicable to both male and female faces). Figures 2 and 3 show the 100 points on the faces (one for males and another for females). These numbers indicate the age, the fortune of which is influenced by the facial features in those areas. Elaboration on the relationship of the name, the age and the destiny are given in subsequent pages.

As shown in Figure 1, the ears are named *lun* 轮. Sometimes a face reader may be more detailed and break down the parts of the ear into *tian lun* 天轮, *tian cheng* 天成 and *tian guo* 天郭. The reason the ears are named *tian lun* 天轮 (meaning heavenly wheel) is that the fortune bestowed on a child from ages 1 to 7 or even to fourteen is pre-determined. The child most likely will not have worked and earned a good fortune. Of course, there are exceptions. But most children are still dependent from ages 1 to 14. Fortunate children usually have well developed ears. Children who experience hardships may have deformed or under-developed ears. Some face readers classify long ears as a sign of longevity, and soft or flexible ears as a sign of weakness in decision making. Some regard high-set ears (where the top of the ear is higher than the eyebrow) as a sign of

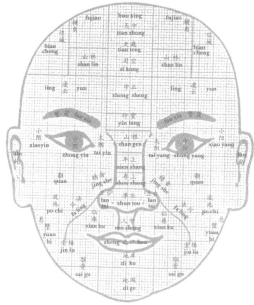

Figure 1. The different areas of the face that influence the fortunes of a person at different ages.

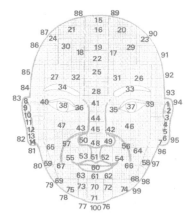

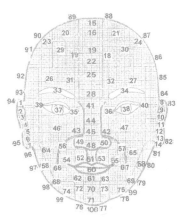

Figure 2. Numbers indicate the age, the fortune of which is influenced by that area of face for males.

Figure 3. Numbers indicate the age, the fortune of which is influenced by that area of face for females.

intelligence. Ears that reflect a balanced personality do not stick out.

On the 14 April 2008, *The Straits Times* reported about a 16 year old boy who killed his 24-year-old lover's husband under her instruction. As the boy was underaged at the time of trial, he escaped the death penalty but has been detained indefinitely. This misfortune is reflected in his unusual ears that stick out prominently.

Huo xing 火星 (the top part of the forehead), which depicts the destiny of age 15, should be regular in form, smooth in profile and without marks, pimples or cuts. It is better that the *huo xing* is not hidden by hair.

A good example would be the incumbent President of Russia (2008) Vladimir Putin. He has a very good *huo xing* on his high forehead, which reflects his intelligence and success; his blue calm eyes reflecting his confidence and inner strength. He became President of Russia at the age of 48. This success is reflected by his well-shaped nose. Similarly, Japanese famous architect, Minori Yamasaki, has a high forehead and a well-formed, successful nose. Karl Marx (1818–1883) also had a very high forehead and prominent facial features such as busy eyebrows and cheek bones.

Tian zhong 天中, the upper forehead below *huo xing*, depicts the luck of age 16 should be full and smooth. Although its bone structure can be slightly concave, the *tian ting* 天庭 (mid forehead below *tian zhong*) should also be smooth and free from moles. Similarly, *fu Jiao*

An impression of Mr Vladimir Putin.

An impression of Mr Minori Yamasaki.

An impression of Karl Marx.

辅角 (right and left upper temples) and *bian cheng* 边城 (right and left upper outer temples) should also be smooth and free from marks and moles. The bone structure of the entire forehead should be slightly concave (see chapter on foreheads page 51–56).

The *zhong zheng* 中正 (lower forehead) is quite a prominent part of the forehead. It denotes the luck of age 25 and of one's profession and career. It should be free from deformity, black spots and blemishes. It should also be even in colour and should not protrude or be sunken.

Yin tang 印堂 (the area between the eyebrows) corresponds to luck during the age of 28. It is sometimes called *ming tang* 命堂 because it refers to a critical point in life: possibly starting a career. Any defective marks or deformity indicate difficulties and ill health that threaten life.

The *Shan lin* 山林 (the right and left lower temples) reveals the luck for the age of 30. Defects that occur on this area depict failure and poor luck. Above the eyebrows and just below the *Shan lin* are the *ling yun* 凌云, which together with the *fan xia* 繁霞 (eyebrows), depict the wellbeing of ages 31 to 34, the quality of life and longevity. Females should have eyebrows that are long, arched and refined. Males should have eyebrows that are long, hairy and well-formed (see chapter on eyebrows pages 57–64).

The destiny of ages 35 to 40 is depicted by the eyes. If the eyelids are thick, financial inheritance may be quite substantial. Generally eyes should be well-shaped and clear (see chapter on eyes, pages 65–74). *Tai yin* 太阴 and *tai yang* 太阳 refer to the inner corner of the right eye and inner corner of the left eye respectively. They should be well-set and clear of moles and defects. If they are bulging or deformed, they indicate a short life span. The eyes should be free from green or red veins. The right and left eye balls are named *zhong yin* and *zhong yang* respectively. They should be sharp and spirited. Individuals whose eyes show more sclera (whites of the eye) than iris (coloured part of the eye) are believed to experience emotional problems. The eyes are said to be the window to the soul, and they do 'speak' and emote more than other facial features. Dark rings or eye bags beneath the eyes could be indicative of lack of sleep or health problems related to the heart. Some believe eyes slanting downwards are able to see spirits. Face readers prefer eyes slightly slanting upward. Leaders of past revolutions have had thick and sometimes slanting eyebrows. Examples of such leaders are: Huang Chou (he led the revolution against the Tang dynasty army in 875), Fang La (he was a revolutionist leader against the North Song in AD 1120), and Russian revolution leader, Ajiekcah Hbahobny Tepueh (1812–1870).

An impression of Ajiekcah Hbahobny Tepueh

The eyebrows depict the fortune or misfortune from the age of 33 to 34, and the area above them indicates one's fate from the ages of 25 to 32. For instance, the 24-year-old woman who incited her 16-year old lover to kill her husband (as reported by *The Straits Times* on 14 April, 2008) has an unusual face, in particular, imbalanced eyebrows. She was sentenced to a 9-year jail term (during her age of 24 to 33).

George Clooney is a super star of many great achievements in Hollywood. His facial features are good and reflect his destiny to be successful. He became successful as young as 19 and by 38 he was already very successful as a producer, and television and film actor.

An impression of Mr George Clooney.

The fortunes of ages 41 to 50 is revealed by the shape and structure of the nose. The area of nose between the eyes is called *shan gen* 山根 and depicts the luck of age 41. A high *shan gen* depicts egotistic characteristics and a low one indicates low self-esteem. Freckles on this area depict impatience. The left and right *jing she* 精舍 (areas of face above wings of the nose) depict the luck of the age of 42. If they are greenish or greyish, calamity may befall the person. The *nian shang* 年上 (area of nose below *shan gen*) and *shou shang* 寿上 (area of nose below *nian shang*) are important areas as they are in the middle portion of the nose that represents luck and ability. They should be sizeable and well-shaped (see chapter on nose, pages 75–85). A straight and strong *nian shang* portrays ability and good fortune, whereas a crooked or soft one could mean ill luck and complacency. Generally, *shan gen* and *shou shang* are related to health. Lines running across or patches of discolouration could result in health problems or set backs in life.

The two *lan tai* 兰台 , or nose wings, represent wealth. Broad and thick nose wings depict fortune or a good career path. Upturned nostrils are not favourable as they could mean overspending.

Xian ku 仙库 literally means storage from the heavens. It denotes whether the person at that age would have plenty to eat or would enjoy his or her wealth.

The left and right *quan* 颧 (left and right cheeks) depict the luck of ages 46 and 47. *Quan* should be full, prominent and free of defective marks. Its bone should not be too pronounced.

One such example is Ms Pratibha Devisingh Patil, the current President of India, who was elected in 2007. She won her first election when she was 27, and became a member of parliament at 51. This is reflected in her high cheek bones, which depict power. Her high forehead is also indicative of her intelligence—she holds several degrees. Her good looks show her inner virtue, strength and fortitude. She also has a well defined *ren zhong*.

The *zhun tou* 准头 (the tip of the nose) is an important part of the nose depicting the destiny at 48. It should be round, well-developed and fleshy. A thin and weak *zhun tou* translates into poverty and disappointment. A hooked *zhun tou* depicts a vicious nature. The right and left wings of the nose, known as *Lan tai* 兰台, should be well-shaped so that the nostrils are not exposed (see chapter on nose pages 75–85).

The ages of 51 to 57 (see chapter on mouth, pages 86–96) are influenced by the areas surrounding the mouth. *Ren zhong* 仁中 (depression above upper lip) should be deep, balanced and well-shaped, this embodies longevity and good fortune at the age of 51. A good example would be

An impression of Ms Pratibha Devisingh Patil.

former Chinese leader, Deng Xiao Ping. The luck from age 52 to 55 is reflected on the areas to the left and right of the *ren zhong*. These areas, the *xian ku* 仙庫, should be well-formed without protrusions or depressions.

An impression of Mr Deng Xiao Ping. He had a well formed ren zhong and strong chin that confirmed his success until a mature age.

An example of this would be when I was in the United States in 1990 promoting Singapore by conducting free face reading sessions, and radio and television interviews. One lady had lines across her *ren zhong* and she encountered problems in her life. I read over a hundred American faces. Ninety percent of people I read gave me positive feedback that my readings were quite accurate.

The tip of the nose is called *zhun tou* which reveals the inner nature of the person. Face readers prefer noses that are fleshy or bulbous because these noses are believed to be signs of good luck and intelligence. A hooked nose is believed to reveal a cunning nature.

The left and right *fa ling* 法令 (lines on the inner cheeks) depict the luck of ages 56 and 57 and one's life span. They should be fairly deep and pronounced at the ages of 56 and 57.

An impression of former Prime Minister of Japan, Shinzo Abe.

A good example is Mr Junichiro Koizumi. He has a distinguished face. He comes from a distinguished family and is a very capable person. As young as 29 he was elected a member of the Lower House and has enjoyed a successful career as a politician. At the age of 58 he became the Prime Minister of Japan. Former Japanese Prime Minister, Shinzo Abe, also has a face with very good features. His ears are well formed and this reflects his good family background; he was born into a political family of significance. His nose, *ren zhong* and *xian ku* are well proportioned and he became Prime Minister at the age of 52.

Another example is Mr Gordon Brown who took office as the Prime Minister of the United Kingdom of Great Britain and Northern Ireland in June 2007. He has good

An impression of Mr Gordon Brown.

An impression of Amadeus Mozart.

facial features that depict success, talent and fame. His *quan* portrays his success when he was 46, when he became the Chancellor of the Exchequer. His *fa ling* are very well formed, so it is no wonder that at the age of 56 he became the Prime Minister.

Similarly, prolific Austrian music composer of the 18th century, Amadeus Mozart, had a very prominent jaw and chin. He showed great talent at the age of three. His first work was published when he was seven, and he had composed great symphonies by age 11. His short *ren zhong* could explain his relatively short life.

The mouth governs luck at age 60 (see chapter on mouth, pages 86–96). Lips should be red and its thickness should be balanced, otherwise it could mean that the person may not live a very long life. Balanced lips with good colour point towards brilliance and fame. Teeth should be even and not protruding, concave or convex. Even the number of teeth signifies luck or ill fortune. For males it is good to have 31 teeth (a *yang* number) but for females it is not so (30, a *yin* number, is better).

An example is John Lee Hooker, the world's greatest Blues singer, who passed away in his sleep at the age of 74. He had prominent and wide lips that reflected his singing ability. He had over 30 labels over a span of 50 years of success. He had a wide and high forehead and his eyes were not as close as normal reflecting his generous nature.

The 74th United States Secretary of Treasury, Henry M. Paulson, ,a key player in the 2008 financial crisis US$700 billion bail out plan, gratuated with an MBA from Harvard Business School in his early 20s and went on to achieve early success when he became Assistant Secretary of Defence at the Pentagon. This is reflected by his high and well-formed forehead. He became a partner of Goldman Sachs in his mid 30s. This is shown by his intelligent and well- proportioned eyes. His success during his mid 40s is reflected by his nose. He has long *ren zhong* that represents longevity and success. His balanced lips shows his success at 60.

The cheeks and chin reveal the destiny of a person from the ages of 58 to 81 (with the exception of age 60). The areas known as the *xuan bi* 悬壁(the part of cheek below the ear) govern the destiny of 58 and 59. These areas should be full and the colour even (without freckles) to indicate good health and luck. The wellbeing of ages 61 to 63 is depicted on the *di ku* 地库(area below mouth). It should be full and fair in colour. The luck of 64 and 65 is spelt out by the areas immediately outside the left and right *fa ling*. If there are lines crossing these areas then there may be problems that take one by surprise. *Po chi*, these areas at age 64 and 65 are better fleshy than skinny.

The left and right *jin lu* 金缕 (the lower tips of *fa ling*) indicate the wellbeing at the ages of 66 and 67. They should be full, not be crossed by lines, and point upwards rather than downwards. The left and right jaws depict the luck at 68 and 69 respectively. These areas should not have green or grey patches on them.

The destiny of ages 70 to 73 is revealed on the chin. This area should be well-formed and free from defects (see chapter on cheeks and chin pages 97–100). From the age of 74 to 75 a person's luck is assessed by looking at the left and right *sai gu* 腮骨(jaw bones) which should be neither too narrow nor too broad. If they are so large or broad that they can be seen from the back of the face, they indicate stubbornness and possible cruelty.

The 74th United States Secretary of Treasury, Henry M. Paulson.

The Face

According to Chinese beliefs, the countenance depicts the emotions and passions of man but the shape, form and proportion of the skull show his intellectual power and sensibility. Even though man ages with passing years and his face wrinkles, his skull remains basically unchanged.

Some face readers classify faces into five types according to the Five Elements namely Gold, Wood, Water, Fire and Earth. Gold faces are roundish, Wood rectangular or oblong, Water irregular, Fire triangulated and Earth squarish.

The Wood face is a elongated face with a long nose and high forehead. Wood is a symbol of growth. Such a face indicates leadership potential, the ability to shoulder much responsibility and a willingness to work hard. A person with a Wood face should keep his or her liver and gall bladder healthy. He or she should also be wary of digestive problems and drink lots of water to avoid gallstones.

The Fire face has narrow but prominent cheekbones, pointed a chin and forehead. Typical Fire Element facial features show warmth and spirit and people with the Fire face are goalsetters. They like nourishing foods and herbs.

The Earth face is typically squarish with distinct jawlines. Those with the Earth face are usually practical, persevering, humane and reliable. They often suffer from stomach and spleen disorders. A diet with less sugar and dairy intake is suitable.

The Gold face is generally oval with pronounced cheekbones and a light complexion. A Gold face has bright, energetic eyes. They make good lawyers, managers or counsellors. They are determined, focused, goal-driven, creative and perceptive. They like good quality food and minerals supplements.

A person with a Water element face usually has a round and soft face. His or her eyes are usually large and shiny. They make good counsellors as they are sensitive and caring. They must take care to maintain healthy kidneys; and should avoid overworking, worrying, drinking too much coffee. They should also avoid eating too much rich food and drink lots of water.

Hong Kong actor Chou Yuen Fatt has a tong face and thoughtful and expressive eyes.

The more detailed approach, however, is to classify faces into 10 desirable shapes of the face, namely, *feng, mu, shen, tian, tong, wang, jia, yong, yuan* and *you*. These 10 shapes can be broadly divided into three general shapes, namely, square, triangular, and oval or round. Square-shaped faces include *feng, mu, tian, tong, wang* and *yong*. Triangular faces include *jia* and *you* while oval are *shen* and *yuan*. Irregularly shaped or deformed faces are considered undesirable.

Singaporean actress Ling Li Yun has a jia face.

Generally it is believed that people with square-shaped faces have positive and dynamic personality traits. Elongated faces indicate creativity, positiveness and confidence. People with narrow faces are creative and artistic, whereas round-faced people are known to be financial wizards.

Charts 2 and 3 (page 32) show the areas of the face, for females and males respectively, to refer to regarding luck and destiny from the ages of 1 to 75. These charts should be read together with Figures 1, 2 and 3 on page 20.

Chart 2: Areas Influencing Fortune and Destiny of Females from Ages 1–75

Age	Area of Face
1 to 7	right *lun* 轮 (right ear)
7 to 14	left *lun* (left ear)
15	*huo xing* 火星 (top of forehead)
16 to 19	*tian zhong* 天中 (upper forehead) to *tian ting* 天庭 (mid forehead)
20	right *fu jiao* 辅角 (right upper temple)
21	left *fu jiao* (left upper temple)
22	*si kong* 司空 (lower middle forehead)
23	right *bian cheng* 边城 (right upper outer temple)
24	left *bian cheng* (left upper outer temple)
25	*zhong zheng* (lower forehead)
26 & 31	right *ling yun* 凌云 (area above right eyebrow)
27 & 32	left *ling yun* (area above left eyebrow)
28	*yin tang* 印堂 (area between eyebrows)
29	right *shan lin* 山林 (right lower temple)
30	left *shan lin* 山林 (left lower temple)
33	right *fan xia* 繁霞 (right eyebrow)
34	left *fan xia* 繁霞 (left eyebrow)
35	*tai yang* 太阳 (inner corner of right eye)
36	*tai yin* 太阴 (inner corner of left eye)

37	*zhong yang* 中阳 (right eye)
38	*zhong yin* 中阴 (left eye)
39	*xiao yang* 小阳 (outer corner of right eye)
40	*xiao yin* 小阴 (outer corner of left eye)
41	*shan gen* 山根 (area of nose between the eyes)
42	right *jing she* 精舍 (area above right wing of nose)
43	left *jing she* (area above left wing of nose)
44	*nian shang* 年上 (area of nose below *shan gen*)
45	*shou shang* 寿上 (area of nose below *nian shang*)
46	right *quan* 颧 (right cheek)
47	left *quan* (right cheek)
48	*zhun tou* 准头 (tip of nose)
49	right *lan tai* (right wing of nose)
50	left *lan tai* 兰台 (left wing of nose)
51	*ren zhong* 仁中 (depression above upper lip)
52 & 54	right *xian ku* 仙库 (right area above upper lip)
53 & 55	left *xian ku* (left area above upper lip)
56	right *fa ling* 法令 (line on right inner cheek)
57	left *fa ling* (line on left inner cheek)
58	right *xuan bi* 悬壁 (area of cheek below right ear)
59	left *xuan bi* (area of cheek below left ear)
60	*zheng kou* 正口 (mouth)
61 to 63	*di ku* 地库 (area below lower lip)
64	right *po chi* 波池 (area on right of right *fa ling*)
65	left *po chi* (area on left of left *fa ling*)
66	right *jin lu* 金娄 (tip of right *fa ling*)
67	left *jin lu* (tip of left *fa ling*)
68	right *gui lai* 归来 (area below right *jin lu*)
69	left *gui lai* (area below left *gui lai*)
70 to 73	*di ge* 地阁 (chin)
74 to 75	*sai gu* 腮骨 (areas flanking *di ge*)

Chart 3: Areas Influencing Fortune and Destiny of Males aged 1–75

Age	Area of Face
1 to 7	left *lun* (left ear)
7 to 14	right *lun* (right ear)
15	*huo xing* 火星 (top of forehead)
16 to 19	*tian zhong* 天中 (upper forehead) to *tian ting* 天庭 (mid forehead)
20	left *fu jiao* 辅角 (left upper temple)
21	right *fu jiao* (right upper temple)
22	*si kong* 司空 (lower middle forehead)
23	left *bian cheng* 边城 (left upper outer temple)
24	right *bian cheng* (right upper outer temple)
25	*zhong zheng* (lower forehead)
26 & 31	left *ling yun* 凌云 (area above left eyebrow)
27 & 32	right *ling yun* (area above right eyebrow)
28	*yin tang* 印堂 (area between eyebrows)
29	left *shan lin* 山林 (left lower temple)
30	right *shan lin* (right lower temple)
33	left *fan xia* 繁霞 (left eyebrow)
34	right *fan xia* (right eyebrow)
35	*tai yang* 太阳 (inner corner of left eye)
36	*yai yin* 太阴 (inner corner of right eye)
37	*zhong yang* 中阳 (left eye)
38	*zhong yin* 中阴 (right eye)
39	*xiao yang* 小阳 (outer corner of left eye)
40	*xiao yin* 小阴 (outer corner of right eye)
41	*shan gen* 山根 (area of nose between the eyes)

42	left *jing she* 精舍 (area above left wing of nose)
43	right *jing she* (area above right wing of nose)
44	*nian shang* 年上 (area of nose below *shan gen*)
45	*shou shang* 寿上 (area of nose below *nian shang*)
46	left *quan* 颧 (left cheek)
47	right *quan* (right cheek)
48	*zhun tou* 准头 (tip of nose)
49	left *lan tai* 兰台 (left wing of nose)
50	right *lan tai* (right wing of nose)
51	*ren zhong* 仁中 (depression above upper lip)
52 & 54	left *xian ku* 仙库 (left area above upper lip)
53 & 55	right *xian ku* (right area above upper lip)
56	left *fa ling* 法令 (line on left inner cheek)
57	right *fa ling* (line on right inner cheek)
58	left *xuan bi* 悬壁 (area of cheek below left ear)
59	right *xuan bi* (area of cheek below right ear)
60	*zheng kou* 正口 (mouth)
61 to 63	*di ku* 地库 (area below lower lip)
64	left *po chi* 波池 (area on left of left *fa ling*)
65	right *po chi* (area on right of right *fa ling*)
66	left *jin lu* 金缕 (tip of left *fa ling*)
67	right *jin lu* (tip of right *fa ling*)
68	left *gui lai* 归来 (area below left *jin lu*)
69	right *gui lai* (area below right *jin lu*)
70 to 73	*di ge* 地阁 (chin)
74 to 75	*sai gu* 腮骨 (areas flanking *di ge*)

The significance of each of the classified shapes in Chinese face reading is listed in Chart 4.

Chart 4: Significance of Face Shapes

Shapes	Significance
feng 风	• intelligence • reliability • practicality • assertiveness • stubbornness • endurance
mu 目	• strength of character • resourcefulness • assertiveness • creativity
tian 田	• endurance • stability • conscientiousness • forthrightness
tong 同	• steadfastness • kindness • faithfulness • endurance
wang 王	• dedication • persistence • discipline • success • achievement
yong 用	• ambition • dependence • apprehension • sensitivity
jia 甲	• intelligence • imagination • patience • ambition • intuitivity
you 由	• independence • self-assurance • assertiveness • demanding
shen 申	• intelligence • luck • determination • flexibility • dynamism • strength
yuan 圆	• wealth • happiness • kindness • tact • spirituality

The *feng* face is wide and appears quite squarish and short. It is characteristic of one who has a high level of intelligence and endurance. This person may also be stubborn and assertive. Few with a *feng* face are known to give up their plans or are found unreliable. My favourite actress Angela Lansbury, (see impression below, right) of *Murder She Wrote* fame, has a *feng* face.

The *mu* face reveals one who has strength of character, is assertive, resourceful and creative. It is slightly rectangular and long. One who has a *mu* face is a good leader and diplomat. They are usually respected for their inventive ideas and creative work. They are also known to be achievers and suited for careers in research and public or social works. The late Chinese premier Zhou Enlai had a *mu* face, so does Hong Kong actor Kenny Bee.

The *tian* face is squarish with wide jaws and temples. It depicts one who has great endurance and fortitude, with a conscientious and forthright nature. Many good soldiers and military leaders have *tian* faces. Some may prefer to lead a quiet life and they are usually calm and composed. Few women have *tian* faces. An unusual example is Hong Kong actress Zhang Man Yu.

The *tong* face is almost rectangular. It belongs to one who is kind, humane, faithful and loyal. People with *tong* faces are also steadfast in their work, calm and able to endure hardship. Hong Kong actors Zhang Zhao Hui and Chow Yuen Fatt (pictured on page 29) have *tong*-shaped faces.

The *wang* face is rectangular with a prominent forehead and chin. It is characteristic of those who are dedicated to and persistent in their pursuit of excellence. People who have *wang* faces are usually natural leaders, disciplined, and resourceful, usually succeeding in their work. Hong Kong actor Wang Shu Chi has a *wang* face.

 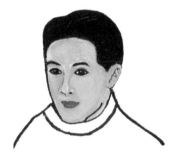

People with *yong*-shaped faces, which are long and narrow, are usually resourceful, creative and assertive. They are not terribly good at concealing hurt feelings. Few people have a *yong* face because it is slightly irregular. American actor John Carradine had a *yong* face.

 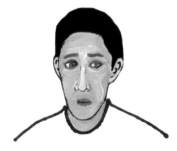

The *jia* face is reflective of one who is intelligent and intuitive. The *jia* face has a wide forehead and a narrow jaw. Those with *jia* faces are sensitive and imaginative. They are also ambitious and aim high. Hong Kong actress Zhou Hai Mei and Singapore actress Lin Liyun (pictured on page 29) both have *jia* faces.

The *you* face characteristically has a narrow forehead and a wide jaw. Those with *you* faces are independent, confident and assertive. They are also usually happy and relaxed. Multi-talented Hong Kong actress, Lydia Sum, had a *you* face.

 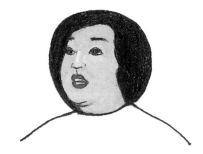

The *shen* face has prominent cheek bones but a pointed and small chin, which is characteristic of intelligent, determined, dynamic and reliable people. They are also flexible and adaptable. American actress Brooke Shields has a *shen* face.

The *yuan* face is round and sometimes slightly plump. It is reflective of those who are kind, tactful and contented. They are also usually positive. Singer Li Lan Feng has a *yuan* face.

Although the 10 shapes of the human face have been listed, there are numerous variations and combinations of the listed shapes. For example, there are shapes that are a combination of *feng* and *mu*, *tian* and *tong*, *wang* and *yong*, *jia* and *mu*, *you* and *feng*, and so on. A combination of face shapes means a combination of characteristics.

Although most people do not have perfectly symmetrical faces, few have obviously asymmetrical ones. Asymmetry can come in various forms, such as imbalanced ear positions, unlevel eyebrows, twisted noses, poorly aligned mouth/lips, imbalanced or protruding jaws. These features are not considered as desirable features.

Retired tennis star, Bjorn Borg, whose three facial zones are almost equal.

The face can be divided into three zones: the upper zone which is the upper part of the face just before the eyebrows, the middle zone which ranges from the eyebrows to the tip of the nose, and the lower zone which runs from the tip of the nose to the chin (refer to Figure 4 on page 41).

The upper zone indicates the mental and intellectual capacity of a person and his or her luck from the age of 15 to 30. The middle zone denotes fortune and capability and the luck of a person from ages 31 to 50. The lower

Evelyn Lip's face at 18 shows the spirit of her eyes. The three areas of her face are almost perfectly equal.

zone denotes financial security and wellbeing after the age of 50. The three zones should be equal in height. A good example would be retired tennis star, Bjorn Borg (pictured top), whose three facial zones are almost equal.

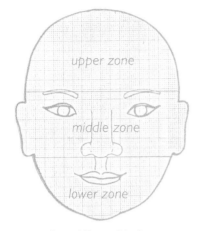
Figure 4. Zones of the Face

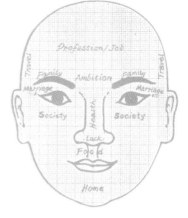
Figure 5. Facial Regions and the Spheres of their Influence

In addition to the three zones, the face is further divided into eight regions, each region governing an aspect of life. The eight regions and their spheres of influence are listed below and shown in Figure 5.

1 Forehead—profession and job
2 *Yin tang* (area between the eyebrows)—ambition
3 *Ling yun* (areas above eyebrows)—family
4 *Xiao yin* and *xiao yang* (outer tips of right and left eyes respectively)—marriage
5 *Quan* (cheeks)—society
6 Nose—health and luck
7 Areas above and below mouth (including chin)—food and home
8 *Qian yi* (left and right sides of forehead)—travel

• The forehead governs the career, profession and how the person gets on with his job. Achievement, accomplishments and success are depicted by a smooth and well-formed forehead. An indented forehead or deformed forehead indicates slow progress and advancement in career. (See well-formed foreheads of Mahatma Gandhi, Margaret Thatcher and Charles Dickens, on page 52).

- *Yin tang*, the area between the eyebrows, governs the ambition and drive of a person. This is an important area because with drive and perseverance, one is likely to succeed. It should be smooth, wide and without defects or marks. Narrow or deformed *yin tang* indicates easy sociability, lack of interest and setbacks in life. *Yin tang* with wild hair depicts a selfish and unforgiving nature that can lead to negativity and a lack of ambition.

- The areas above the eyebrows should be free from marks that mar or disfigure. These areas govern family life, filial piety and love between family members. They also reveal family influence and inheritance. If there are deformities or marks, the person may not have good family support.

- The outer tips of the left and right eyes govern marital happiness. Defects occurring on these areas may indicate problems concerning marriage partners.

- The *quan,* or cheeks, indicate how society treats the person and how he or she interacts with his or her friends. If the cheek bones are strong and well-formed, the person makes good lasting friendship with people and enjoys rapport and support from his or her friends and superiors.

- The nose depicts the health and luck of a person. Deformities and wrinkles on the nose indicates poor health and ill luck. An extremely thin nose with exposed nostrils indicates ill luck and empty bank accounts.

- The areas above and below the mouth relate to the home life, which includes food and comfort. If these areas are deformed, the person could suffer emotionally from having a broken home or may experience hardship in life.

- The *qian yi* or sides of the forehead depict how much a person travels and gains experience and wealth from overseas ventures.

The Qin dynasty encyclopedia, *Gu Jin Tu Shu Zhi Cheng*, dated 1726, has the following record on face reading:

大凡观人之相貌。
眉目之清秀。
看神气之荣枯。
取手足之厚薄。
观须发之疏浊。

Translated, it means: in face reading, read the clarity and refinement of the eyes and eyebrows; look for the glow or the withering of *shen qi* (spirit and energy) and examine the hands and feet to see if they are thick, look for the scarcity or abundance of hair and beard.

FACE READING AND HEALTH

Huang Di Nei Jing (Yellow Emperor's Internal Classic) is the seminal medical text of ancient China. It was compiled over a long period but was recorded during the 7th century AD. *Huang Di Nei Jing* states that the health of one's internal organs (such as the heart, the spleen, the liver, the lungs and the kidneys) can be observed from facial features because both the internal and external organs of the human body are interlinked by the meridian, channels through which the life force, known as *qi*, flows.

When a traditional Chinese medicine doctor examines a patient with a chronic illness, he gets him to relate how he feels. He makes observations on the patient's health

by examining the colour and coating of his tongue; and the colour and expression of the face. He also tries to assess and detect *qi* in the patient's body. *Qi* is the breath of life. When there is sufficient *qi* in the body, the face shows a rosy colour , and the eyes will be full of life and bright. Insufficient *qi* causes the body to be lethargic and fatigued, and the eyes dull. *Qi* channels are called meridians. There are 12 main meridians that correspond with 12 major internal organs of the body. The key organs associated with blood are the heart, liver, and spleen. The key organs involved in the distribution and excretion of body fluids are the lungs, spleen, and kidneys. *Qi* flows through the meridians and organs for good health to be maintained.

The kidney and the ears are Water Elements. Indicators of kidney disease may be visible on the forehead and ears, in the form of rashes or a greyish colour. Besides this, the individual may encounter a bitter taste in the mouth; the tip of the tongue will be red with a thin yellow coating.

Respiratory failure or lung diseases are reflected on the nose. The lungs and nose are related, and are of the Gold Element. Redness, puffiness and breakouts around the nostrils and lower cheek may indicate the consumption of too many dairy products that can produce mucus and congestion in the lungs.

The spleen, lips and the mouth are associated with the Earth Element. Symptoms of spleen disease include fever, heart palpitations, and ulcerations of the mouth. The Earth Element affects Gold adversely. The nose is of Gold Element. Some people with illnesses relating to the spleen may also suffer from nosebleeds.

The mouth reflects the energy of the stomach and intestines. The lower part of the face relates to the lower abdomen. White spots or a granular-like feeling under the skin and blotchy areas may point to yeast infection, or too much dairy or sugar in the diet. If the lower lip protrudes, this may be due to a weak digestive system and if the top lip is cracked, red, or has spots at the corner, this could indicate stomach acidity or heat caused by an inappropriate diet.

If the chin is red and swollen, it could indicate a structural weakness in the organs, candida or stuck *qi* in the abdomen. Lines that run down the cheek from the inner corner of the eye may point to a bowel problem. A yellow colour around the mouth and lack of tone in the mouth indicate that the digestive energy is weak and a change of diet and enzymes are needed. A greenish colour indicates that the liver is the prime cause of the problem.

The heart, the forehead, the eyebrows and the tongue are related and are of the Fire Element. Heart illnesses start with a shortness of breath. Numerous lung conditions can also produce shortness of breath. When the forehead suddenly has lots of pimples or discoloured spots, it could be time to see a doctor for a proper check up.

Thyroid problems are indicated by eyebrows that dissipate at the ends.

Liver disorders may be caused by the abnormal storage of metals in the liver leading to tissue damage. The liver and the eyes are of Wood Element and so one of the symtoms of diseased liver can be seen in the corneas of their eyes. Small spider-like veins in the skin may also be found.

The elements present in a face indicate the strengths and weaknesses that the person has to deal with in this life; the shape of features set the pattern and timing of events in a life. The zones show current and potential health patterns. So, when reading a face it is important to take each feature within the context of the whole.

The Ears

The ear consists of an inner ear that cannot be seen, and an outer ear that can. The outer ear is analysed in face reading. It is composed of two parts, the bordering and the lobe. Ears are important features because they govern the fortune of ages 1 to 14.

The personal traits as well as destiny for a male from 1 to 7 years old can be assessed by looking at the left ear and from 8 to 14, at the right ear. For a female, the right ear is analysed for ages 1 to 7 and the left, for ages 8 to 14.

The length, shape and profile of the ear are believed to depict the life span, personality traits and ambitions of a person. The longer the ears, the longer the life span and the better fortune enjoyed by the person. This is why Shou Xing, the god of longevity in Chinese mythology, is always portrayed with unusually long ears. It is believed that Buddha, too, had long ear lobes. The shape of the outer circle and the lobe reveal the characteristics of a person.

If the upper portion of the ear is large or larger than the lower portion, it indicates intelligence and a strong memory. If the middle part is wider than the upper and lower parts, it indicates strong creativity and intellectual capacity. If the lowest part is fleshy and as wide or big as the upper parts, it indicates compassion and patience. The shapes of ears identified in face reading are rectangular, pointed, long and round (refer to Chart 5 on page 49).

An impression of Francis Chopin's face.

For instance, renowned Polish pianist and composer, Francis Chopin, had round ears and an expressive, artistic face that revealed his talents.

The length and shape of the ear suggests the personality traits of an individual but the profile and thickness of the helix and lobe depict the luck and good fortune of the person. The fleshier the ear, the more luck and security available. Thin and twisted ears signify poor luck and very badly formed ears depict a disturbed personality.

The shape of the ears is not likely to change over the years although they tend to grow slightly longer. A bend or an irregular deformation on the outer or inner circle of the ear could signify that an unhappy event could happen during the earlier part of one's life.

The position of the ears in relation to the eyebrow height defines the character of the person, as shown in Chart 6 on page 50. The ideal position of ears is just below the height of the eyebrow and just above the tip of the nose.

Ears that are below the eyebrow and above the tip of the nose (see Figure 6 on page 48) indicate that the person is honest, kind, intelligent and patient. A person with ears above the eyebrow is egoistic, hot-tempered, ambitious, determined but highly successful.

Ears that are flattish and do not protrude when the face is examined from the frontal view indicate that the person is kind, dynamic, forgiving and fair. Ears that stick out means that the person may be endowed with wealth but his happiness may be marred by personal conflict.

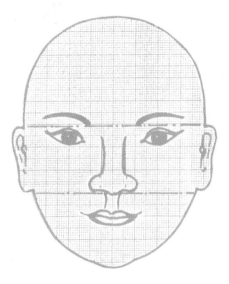

Figure 6. The ideal position of the ear is just below the eyebrow and above the tip of the nose.

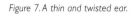

Figure 7. A thin and twisted ear.   *Figure 8. A badly formed ear.*

Chart 5. Shape of the Ear and Corresponding Characterisitics

Shape of Ear		Characteristics
rectangular		• honest • compassionate • intelligent • stable
pointed		• shrewd • sensitive • intuitive • alert
long		• determined • honest • conservative • long life
round		• artistic • creative • good natured • appreciative of cultural activities

However, ears should be proportionate to the face. If the ears are too large, the face would look rather awkward. On the other hand, if the ears are too small, the person may not have the support from others.

Summing up, the shape of the ear should be balanced, close to the head and preferably long and fleshy.

Chart 6: Summary of the Types of Ears and Their Significance

Types of Ears	Significance
ear with good lobe, fleshy, shiny and smooth	• brilliance • luck • good family support • determination
ear with a small lobe and is thin, dull and ill-formed	• dull • poor luck • poor family background • lacking in confidence
ear with long lobe, well-shaped and smooth	• long life • wealth
ear without lobe, very short, dry, poorly formed and irregular	• short life • poverty
ear above level of eyebrows, with good lobe and well-shaped	• wealth • promotion • progress
ear pointed and shaped like a triangle	• greedy • immoral • early death for parents

The Forehead

The forehead reveals the intellect and attitude of a person. It also shows the fortune of ages 15 to 32. Some face readers are able to read how vivid a person's imagination is, how good is his memory and how powerful his observation of details by looking at his forehead. Imaginative and observant people have rounded and prominent foreheads.

There are basically two types of profiles for foreheads: concave and convex. The convex, broad and high forehead indicates positive, efficient, intelligent and imaginative characteristics. Many musicians and highly intelligent people have convex and broad foreheads. The world's famous Broadway composer, Andrew Lloyd Webber, composer of the music of the *Phantom of the Opera,* has a convex forehead. Other famous examples are listed on the following page. On the other hand the concave, narrow and low forehead is indicative of a patient, agreeable and easygoing person.

A convex, broad
and high forehead.

A concave, narrow
and low forehead.

Former Indian political leader, Mr Mahatma Gandhi, also had a convex face, great resolute nose and benevolent forehead. His thoughtful eyes and large ears depicted his compassion for others and his long life.

The great English novelist, Charles Dickens, had a broad and high forehead that reflected his intellectual creativity.

Former British Prime Minister, Mrs Margaret Thatcher, has a slightly convex and distinguished face. Her nose is well formed. It is not surprising she became leader of the Conservative Party and then Prime Minister at 50 and 54 respectively.

There are a few variations of foreheads such as broad, narrow, high, low and average in size. The ideal size of a forehead is ⅓ that of the face, as seen in the sketch below.

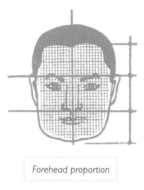

Forehead proportion

If the three parts of the face are unequal or imbalanced, the person's judgement of things or situations may also be imbalanced. Refer to the image below. Chart 7 (page 54) shows some typical foreheads and their significance.

On 4 November 2008, Mr Obama was elected to become the 44th president of the USA. His facial features (balanced lips, facial proportion and strong chin) portray his calm nature, his determination, his drive in life and his talents.

Chart 7. Typical Foreheads and Their Significance

Type		Significance
high and broad		• intellectual • creative • practical • virtuous • forgiving • generous
high and narrow		• intellectual • practical • cautious • imaginative
average		• intelligent • balanced • inventive • compassionate • sociable • practical
low and broad		• practical • athletic • robust
low and narrow		• strong minded • not very compassionate • preferring outdoor life

Regardless of the types of foreheads, the profile of the forehead should be convex, full and free of defective marks. Creases on the forehead just above the eyebrows may be indicative of worries. Many successful people have a single crease above the eyebrows. Horizontal lines on the forehead are favourable especially those with three unbroken lines. Many world leaders and highly successful people have these lines. The Chinese have a saying that *san hua cheng wang* (a person who has three lines on the forehead will become king).

When I was interviewed by a TV network in New York on face reading, the interviewers were quite skeptical at the beginning of the programme.

Taiwanese actress Lin Chin Hsia also has a good and high forehead.

I was asked to read their faces before I could explain what face reading was about. But by the end of the programme, the interviewers were convinced that face reading was much more than just an interesting subject. The art of face reading helps people to understand not just one's individuality but also inclination.

Chinese famed artist, Ren Bainien (above) (1840–1896) was much respected for his paintings of birds, figures and landscape. His talents were reflected by his facial features such as a high forehead, long straight nose and sensitive eyes.

Famous scholars, composers, authors and inventors had high foreheads and high nose ridges. Two examples of such scholars are: Huang Zhi (left) (1904–1938) and Lu Xun (right) (1881–1936). Lu Xun was a revolutionist, using his scholaristic and writing talents to reveal the decadance of old Chinese society. His works are famous and remain popular until present times.

The Eyebrows

Eyebrows depict the intellectual and emotional faculties of a person. They also denote the quality of life from ages 33 to 34.

Generally, eyebrows should be longer than the eyes and should be well-formed. Fine, arched eyebrows are feminine, while rectilinear and bushy brows are masculine.

Long and well-formed eyebrows denote intelligence, gentleness and a strong capacity to cultivate scholastic, cultural and social skills. Eyebrows that are much shorter than the eyes or have scars that mar them depict selfish and crude characteristics.

This picture shows a man with drooping eyebrows, and lips turned downward. These features portray a pessimistic personality.

Hua Tuo, the most respected surgeon during the Three Kingdoms era, had drooping eyebrows. He was an able surgeon and he used acupunture to stop pain when he operated on his patients.

The hair of the eyebrows indicates the intelligence and compassion of a person. The hair of the eyebrows should be firm and running parallel. Long eyebrows with fine hair signify inner beauty and strength, compassion and sensitivity, intelligence and capability to perform. Short, bushy eyebrows depict practicality and determination but if the eyebrows are not well-delineated with hair growing in different directions, the character may be hot-tempered and impatient. Interrupted eyebrows (those that are marred by a cut or loss of hair. See top drawing in facing page.) indicate setbacks in life. Wild and overly bushy eyebrows denote a perplexed and wild personality. If the hair of the eyebrow is scarcely grown the person may not be able to keep his savings.

The area of the face between the eyebrows is called *yin tang*. The *yin tang* is preferred to be wide rather than narrow. A wide *yin tang* indicates that the person is broad minded and positive. If it is very narrow, so much so that the eyebrows almost meet, then the person may be negative and unforgiving. A wide *yin tang* could mean that the person may have a volatile personality. The ideal width of the *yin tang* should be the width of two index fingers laid flat.

Wrinkles on the *yin tang* are indicative of a person's character as indicated in Chart 7 (see also Moles and Wrinkles on page 101).

Chart 7. Wrinkles on the Yin Tang and Their Significance

Wrinkles	Significance
	• decisive • positive • ambitious • practical
	• indecisive • negative • temperamental • sensitive

Eyebrows that are too close to the eyes means that the person may be selfish and unforgiving. Below are four types of eyebrows that are considered undesirable.

This eyebrow is not well-formed because the hair is not continuous. It suggests that difficulty will be encountered at the ages of 33 and 34.

This eyebrow is not favourable because another (smaller eyebrow) grows above it. It depicts danger encountered at the ages of 33 and 34.

This eyebrow is too short and too high above the eye. It depicts a weak character and poor luck.

This eyebrow is too wild and too low over the eye, signifying a mean character and introverted tendency.

There are many types of eyebrows. The following nine types are the more typical ones.

The *yue mei* 月眉 denotes intellectual brilliance, compassion, emotion and success. It is refined and slightly arched.

The *yi zhi mei* 一字眉 spells success and harmony. It resembles the word *yi* 一 and is rectilinear, straight and refined. It tapers to a point and is longer than the eye.

The *qing xiu mei* 清秀眉 represents the successful and educated. It is slightly arched, tidy, long and refined, tapering to a point and arching over the eyes.

The *hu mei* 虎眉 represents the powerful and outstanding. It is bushy but well-defined, firm and the hair is of constant length.

The *xiao sao mei* 小扫眉 depicts the lonely and independent. It is bushy looking, much like a brush.

The *jian duan mei* 间断眉 represents the average, idle, mean and unforgiving. It is brownish and is broken or marred.

The *ba zi mei* 八字眉 depicts the frustrated although successful. It is slightly slanting and looks like the character *ba* 八.

The *long mei* 龙眉 is good as it spells a well balanced personality, sociable and friendly. It is straight and well formed.

The *shi zi mei* 狮子眉 spells fortune and happiness. It is bushy but the hair is fine and well formed.

Eyebrows depict the inner strength of a person. People with thick eyebrows are more confident or consistent than those with short or very thin eyebrows. Eyebrows that are sparse or broken depict weakness or problems in life. The following few illustrations and images are examples of wellknown people.

Above: An impression of Hermann Goering, Hitler's air minister, who was sentenced to death for war cirmes at the end of World War II. His eyebrows were very close to his sharp eyes and his lips were very thin.

Below: Singapore singer Anita Sarawak has brilliant eyes and matching eyebrows.

Above: Former Soviet Union leader, Joseph Stalin, had shi zi mei, eyebrows that were bushy but fine and well formed.

Below: Former Pakistan Prime Minister Benazir Bhutto had arched yue eyebrows, brilliant eyes and a mu face.

A face with narrow life palace.

An impression of Aaron Kwok. He is a very talented actor and dancer. His pointed ears show his sensitivity and intuition in what he does. He has very good facial features: a good life palace and an excellent face profile.

This sketch shows my favourite Hong Kong actress. She has a sweet and good-looking face. Her life palace is wide.

The space between the eyebrows is named *ming gong* or life palace and it portrays fate as well as attitude towards life. A small space indicates a negative attitude (refer to the picture of a man with small life palace at the top of this page). On the other hand, a person with a wide life palace probably has a positive and optimistic attitude. Jackie Chan, a famous Hong Kong actor, for example, has a wide life palace. He should have the ability to turn a difficult situation into an easy opportunity. Creases on the life palace may signify many intellectual activities in the past, but too many indicates many worries.

The Eyes

The eyes are analysed for the fortune of ages 35 to 40. It is generally accepted that active and vivid eyes reflect an active and acute mind. The fire in the eyes reveals emotion, compassion and even hatred. This is why some say that the eyes are the windows to the soul. The eyes reveal grief and pleasure, disappointment and triumph, wisdom and ignorance, and all feelings good and bad.

The colours of eyes most common among the Chinese are dark brown and black. The darker the colour, the more intelligent the person. The colour of the eyes of a Caucasian may not be black. It may be green or blue. Intelligence and compassion are revealed by the clarity of colour and the spirit of the eyes. However, the proportion of white compared with the iris (the round coloured part of the eye) is also an important consideration in analysing the eyes. (Refer to sketches below for well-proportioned and ill-proportioned eyes with reference to the 'whites'.)

A well-proportioned eye portrays a balanced personality

An ill-proportioned eye depicts inner conflict and emotion

Lively eyes with fire together with good delineation depict strength, vigour, good health and vivacity.

Generally there are about 40 differently shaped eyes. The more common ones are shown below. Each type is named after an animal, as the Chinese believe that human eyes bear resemblance to animal eyes. Chart 8 (page 68) summarises the different classification of the eyes.

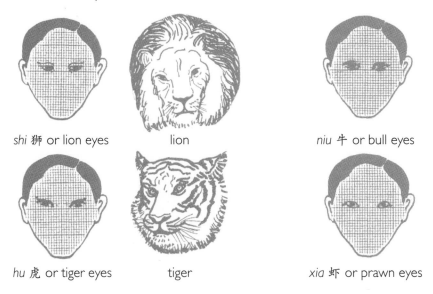

| *shi* 狮 or lion eyes | lion | *niu* 牛 or bull eyes |

| *hu* 虎 or tiger eyes | tiger | *xia* 虾 or prawn eyes |

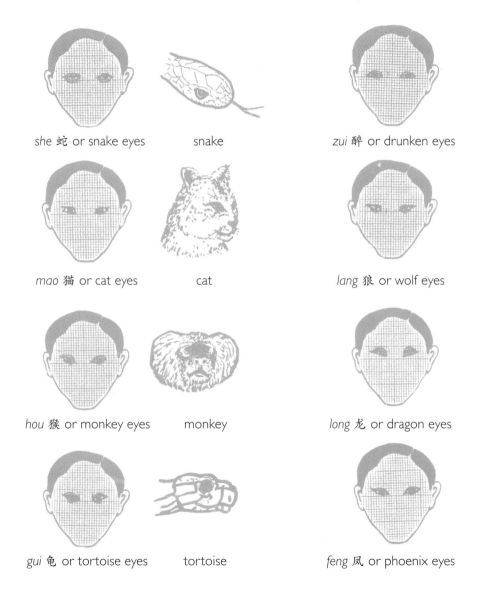

she 蛇 or snake eyes

snake

zui 醉 or drunken eyes

mao 猫 or cat eyes

cat

lang 狼 or wolf eyes

hou 猴 or monkey eyes

monkey

long 龙 or dragon eyes

gui 龟 or tortoise eyes

tortoise

feng 凤 or phoenix eyes

Chart 8. Five Categories of the Various Types of Eyes

Powerful & Intellectual	Sleepy & Inactive	Sensuous & Beautiful	Sharp & Cunning	Honest & Sober
long (dragon)	zui (drunken)	feng (phoenix)	lang (wolf)	niu (cow)
hu (tiger)	gui (tortoise)		she (snake)	mao (cat)
shi (lion)			hou (monkey)	xia (prawn)

The relationship of the eyes to the nose and the eyebrows, the slant of the eyes, the size of the eyes, the distance between the eyes, the profile of the eyelids and the spirit of the eyes, are just as important as the shape of the eyes. Eyes should be well-positioned, slanting slightly upwards. However, eyes that slant too much (see middle illustration below) depict imbalance of temperament and shrewdness. Refer to Chart 9 (page 70) for the positions of eyes and their significance.

The white of the eyes should be clear and not bloodshot. Also, if there are 'three whites' the personality traits may be ultrasensitivity, selfishness and high excitability. This woman (top right) whose eyes have 'three whites' was found guilty of helping her husband to commit murder and was hanged. When the iris is at the bottom or on top and the white of the eye is to the left, right and below or above the eye is classified

When the eyeball floats too high or too low, the eye is classified as having "three whites" which is not a good sign. When there are four whites the person is believed to have a violent temper.

as having three whites. This type of eye, very often, depicts a determined, tactless and hot tempered personality.

Eyes too large in
proportion to face.

Eyes and eyebrows
are too slanting.

Imbalanced eyes (one slants
more than the other).

Eyes too close
to eyebrows.

Eyes slightly slanting.

Eyes too close
together and
eyebrows too short.

Chart 9. Position of the Eyes and Their Significance

Position	Significance
close together	mean
far apart	generous
close to eyebrows	introverted
slanting	shrewd
big (in relation to face)	naive
small (in relation to face)	secretive
deeply set	cautious
protruding	outspoken
dull	lifeless
shifty	shrewd or dishonest

The illustrations in the following pages are a sampling of different eye positions and their significance.

This sketch shows an example of well-delineated, long and spirited eye representing wisdom and intelligence.

Eyes should be positioned not too far apart or too close to the *yin tang*. Some face readers say the eyes with thick lids may have rich inheritance. See sketch below.

Individuals with protruding eye balls may suffer from an ailment. See sketch below.

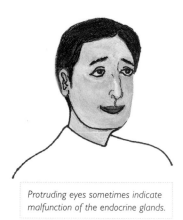

Protruding eyes sometimes indicate malfunction of the endocrine glands.

Drooping eyes often have eyebrows slanting downwards. See sketch below.

A person who has very narrow or constricted eye slits is a cautious person.

A person with a triangulated eye shape is cunning.

Eyeballs should be lively but they should not be overly tense, penetrating or fierce. I did a sketch of my most respected painter Vincent Van Gogh (based on his own self portrait) to show how keen and intense his eyes were. He was said to be overzealous and died at the age of 37.

The Nose

The nose is an important face feature since a person breathes through the nose. When the nose is blocked he suffers and at the very worst, suffocates. This shows how important the nose is in relation to the wellbeing of the person. Face readers regard the nose as the 'hill' of the face, which generates willpower and represents intellectual capabilities. The nose also depicts the fortune of the ages 41 to 50.

Generally, the nose should be fleshy and not thin, showing the bone structure. The nostrils should be hidden by the *lan tai* or the wings of the nose and the *zhun tou* (nose tip). Pointed and thin noses indicate poor luck and poverty. A twisted nose depicts aggressiveness.

There are 20 categories of noses in face reading. Thirteen of them, which are the more common ones are featured here.

Those with the *long bi* 龙鼻, or dragon nose, are very fortunate and successful. The length of the nose is equal to the forehead. The outline of the nose is well-delineated, neither pointed nor too broad. The nostrils are gently shortened. The *nian shang* (bridge) is straight and firm.

The *shi bi* 狮鼻 or lion nose is characteristic of those who are highly successful and wealthy. The length of the nose is equal to the forehead. The outline of the nose is well defined but the end of the nose is fleshy and rounded. The nostrils are hardly visible.

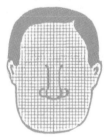

The *hu bi* 虎鼻 or tiger nose signifies fame and wealth. The nose is straight in profile but the nostrils are hardly seen and are gently rounded.

The *dan bi* 胆鼻 or gall bladder nose represents wealth and luck. The nose tip is slightly rounded and the nostrils cannot be seen.

The *yang bi* 羊鼻 or goat nose denotes fame and wealth. The nose is straight but the tip of the nose is fleshy and the nostrils cannot be seen.

The *niu bi* 牛鼻 or bull nose denotes peace and comfort. The nose resembles that of a bull although the nostrils are not as large or as exposed as those of the bull.

The *gou bi* 狗鼻 or dog nose represents compassion for others. The nose is not perfectly straight and the nostrils slightly resemble those of the dog.

The *suan bi* 蒜鼻 or garlic nose spells honour and good retirement. The nose resembles a garlic. The tip of the nose is rounded and small.

The *ying bi* 鷹鼻 or eagle nose denotes treachery and cunning. The nose is pointed and its bridge is not straight. The nostrils are set back.

The *hou bi* 猴鼻 or monkey nose indicates wealth that does not last. The nose is like that of a monkey's with exposed nostrils and skinny, bony bridge.

The *jian bi* 剑鼻 or sword nose represents selfishness and desertion. The bridge resembles a sword as it is very bony. The nostrils are thin and exposed.

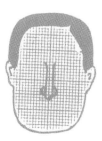

The *yu bi* 鱼鼻 or fish nose reflects hardship and poverty. The nose is pitched very high and the nostrils are large.

The *lu bi* 鹿鼻 or deer nose denotes wealth and popularity. The nose is slightly pointed and rounded. The nostrils are small.

There are certain basic defects that affect all the categories:

• Moles on the nose are generally not good symbols. They mean setbacks or harsh experiences in life.

• Depressions on the bridge of the nose also denote poor luck or calamities.

• Grey patches on the skin or freckles that suddenly appear on certain areas of the nose also spell ill fortune.

• If the wings of the nose (*lan tai*) are imbalanced, the person may lose his savings at the age of 49 or 50.

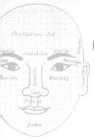
PROFILE OF NOSE

While the shape of the nose viewed from the front generally indicate the fortune of a person, the profile of the nose shows the personality of the person.

This profile is of a person who is dynamic, progressive, domineering, practical and stubborn.

This profile shows that the person is artistic, honest, gentle, imaginative and adaptable.

A person with this nose profile is ambitious, skillful in business, shrewd, practical and materialistic.

A person with this profile is soft hearted, simple minded, contented and unsociable (but if the nostrils are exposed, he or she is extroverted).

SOME NOSES ANALYSED

The nose below has a strong bone structure at the upper half and a well-formed lower half consisting of a rounded *zhun tou* which droops slightly downward. The wings on the sides are well-shaped giving ample surround to the nostrils. The muscles of the face at the sides of the nose (including the cheeks) are well-formed. The nose depicts luck, power, intelligence, assertiveness and conscientiousness. Hong Kong actor Chou Yuen Fatt (pictured on page 29) has well-delineated nose and well-formed wings. They depict intelligence, balanced personality and luck.

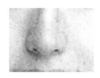

This nose below has a weak root and a convex bridge profile. The *zhun tou* is small and the wings are thin with nostrils exposed. This depicts ill luck, insecurity and pessimism.

The nose shown below has a concave profile and slightly hooked bridge. The *zhun tou* is drooping and appears hooked. The wings are narrow and the nostrils are not seen. This nose reflects exhibitionistic impulse, shrewdness, selfishness and aggression.

Summing up, it can be said that the best type of nose is one that is straight and moderately large with a rounded tip. It should be fleshy with nostrils well-concealed. Its bone structure should be straight and its wings balanced and fleshy. Hong Kong actor, Jackie Chan and the late Duchess of Windsor, Wallis Simpson, all have good and well-shaped noses.

An impression of Hong Kong actor Jackie Chan who has a strong and well-formed nose.

An impression of Wallis Simpson (late Duchess of Windsor). She had a good nose profile.

Dr Sun Yat Sen had facial features that portrayed his compassion, perseverance and principles.

An impression of Poet Ben Jonson. He did not have an easy life but finally when he was 44 he was recognised and honoured for his poems.

The Mouth

Whatever is in the mind of a person is communicated through the mouth. Whatever the heart feels is expressed through the mouth. The Chinese have a proverbial saying *fu cong kou ru, huo cong kou chu* 福从口入，祸从口出，which means that good luck (including food) enters through the mouth and ill luck (including gossip that leads to trouble) exits through the same mouth. This shows how important the mouth is to a person. To the face reader, the mouth (including the areas around it, ie, the *ren zhong*, *fa ling* and *xuan bi*) govern the luck of a person's life from the ages of 51 to 60. There are about 20 types of mouths. Eleven common types are described over the next few pages.

The *si fang kou* 四方口 or square mouth spells fortune and talent. The shape of the mouth is squarish. The upper and lower lips are balanced and the line formed when the mouth is closed is straight. The lips are pinkish red.

The *niu kou* 牛口 or bull mouth denotes wealth and longevity. The shape of the mouth resembles slightly that of the bull. The lips are fleshy and when they are closed a straight line is formed.

The *long kou* 龙口 or dragon mouth represents fortune and high office. The lips form a straight line when closed and they are firm and well-defined.

The *hu kou* 虎口 or tiger mouth reflects power and wealth. The mouth is large and curls up very slightly. The lips are balanced, well-defined and slightly fleshy.

The *yang kou* 羊口 or goat mouth spells poverty. The mouth protrudes slightly and the lips are thin and weak.

The *zhu kou* 猪口 or pig mouth spells ill luck. The mouth is large but the lips are imbalanced. The upper lip protrudes while the lower lip is smaller and set back slightly.

The *yue kou* 月口 or moon mouth represents luck and wealth. The mouth is like a half moon with its ends tilted up slightly denoting an inclination to pleasure.

Gong kou 弓口 or bow mouth denotes wealth and a happy old age. It resembles a bow. The lips are fleshy, pink and proportionate, denoting sensuality and compassion.

The *huo kou* 火口 or fire mouth spells poverty. The lips look like those that are blowing on firewood to start a fire. They are protruding and thin. When closed they form a single line denoting coldness and indifference.

The *tao kou* 桃口 or peach mouth represents sensibility and luck. The lips are as pink as peaches and they are small, indicating innocence and kindness.

The *yu kou* 鱼口 or fish mouth depicts poverty. The mouth is very small and the lips are hardly seen. The lower lips are slightly hollowed in the middle.

THE LIPS

It is believed that the longer the lips, the better the luck and longer the life span. The profile of the upper and lower lips must match. If the upper lip is thin and lower is thick, there is imbalance and the person may also be slightly imbalanced emotionally.

Thin lips are associated with an impulsive, hard-hearted and cold personality. Even lips that are balanced in shape and size, with an upwardly tilted line (formed when the mouth is closed) are a sign of good luck, self-assuredness, contentment, reliability, intelligence, emotional stability and tenderness.

An impression of Iran leader, Mr Mahmond Ahmadinejad. He has firm lips that depict firmness in making decisions.

PROFILE OF LIPS

When the upper lip is cantilevered beyond the lower, the lips portray insecurity, shyness and unassertiveness.

When the upper lip is set back and the lower lip protrudes, the lips portray selfishness and inconsideration.

When the *ren zhong* (depression above the upper lip) is convex in profile and the lips slightly set back, the lips denote selfishness and materialistic tendencies.

When the *ren zhong* is concave in profile and the upper lips protrude, the lips portray indifference and instability in love.

TEETH

Although teeth are not regarded as important as other features in face reading, they should be well-proportioned and of an appropriate size in relation to the mouth. They should be even and balanced in terms of length and spacing.

Protruding teeth are not only ugly but also point to an inability to retain wealth. Teeth that are extremely uneven in size and length signify ill luck.

Well-formed teeth depict well-being and a balanced personality.

Mouth with protruding teeth.

Mouth with irregular teeth.

REN ZHONG

The *ren zhong* is the depression just above the upper lip, which ends at the tip of the nose. The length of the *ren zhong* is said to indicate the life span of the person. The longer it is, the longer life one will have.

Ren zhong, *the groove below the nose tip, depict the life span and health of a person. When it is long it signifies longevity.* Above left: Ren zhong *that resembles the character* ba. Above right: Ren zhong *that resembles an upside down* ba.

Mr Ronald Reagan, former President of the United States of America, had long ears and long ren zhong *that depicted his long and successful life. See the right sketch with long* ren zhong.

If the *ren zhong* resembles the character *ba* 八, the person could encounter a difficult period in his early life. If the *ren zhong* is like an upside down *ba* 丷, it means that he may have a harder time during his old age. *Ren zhong* should be balanced.

Napoleon Bonaparte (left) (1769–1821) was a French political leader, a general during the French revolution. He staged a coup d'etat and declared himself First Council in 1799. Five years later he was crowned emperor. He led his army to invade Russia in 1812. He was defeated and he abdicated in 1814. His attempt to regain control failed and he retreated to the island of St Helena where he died in 1821. His relatively short life was reflected by his short ren zhong. *Similarly, Italian lady artist and architect, Raffaello Sarizio (right) (1483–1520) also had a short* ren zhong.

FA LING

The *fa ling,* the lines on the inner cheeks that frame the mouth, determine one's luck at ages 56 and 57 and indicate if one is filial or not. Good *fa ling* should resemble a bell and be balanced. Imbalanced left and right *fa ling* signifies early separation from parents and family. If moles are found on both *fa ling,* a person may lose the protection of both parents at an early age. Refer to Figures 9 and 10 (page 96) for more.

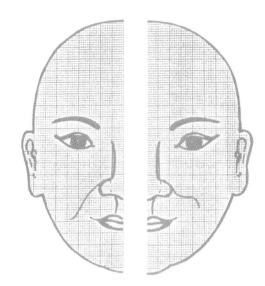

Figure 9. Fa ling that signifies good luck (left) and happiness (right).

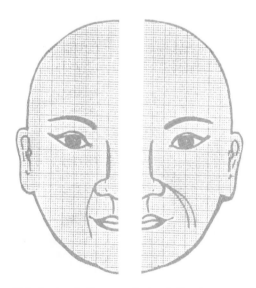

Figure 10. Fa ling that signifies two professions (left) and uncertainty (right).

The Cheeks and Chin

The upper parts of the cheeks reveal the fortune of the ages 46 to 47, while its lower parts show a person's luck during the ages 58 and 59, and from 64 to 67. The chin reveals the fortune of a person from 61 to 75 years of age.

CHEEKS

The upper cheeks should be rounded and well-formed with smooth skin. High cheek bones are considered favourable but they must not be too high either, otherwise a person may be over-dominating, stubborn and proud. High cheek bones also must be accompanied by a strong nose or else success may not come as expected. This is because both the cheeks and nose signify power. Empress Wu Zetian of the Tang dynasty had high cheek bones and she eventually gained supreme power and was able to maintain it for years. Similarly, the late Duchess of Windsor, Wallis Simpson, had a very good face profile (refer to the impression of Wallis Simpson on page 84). The different types of cheek bones and their significance is shown in Chart 10 (page 98).

Chart 10. Cheek Bones and Their Significance

Cheek Bones	Significance
lean and imbalanced	• ill health • shy • undisciplined • relaxed
flat	• pessimistic • reserved • insecure • complacent • easy sociability
high (with strong nose)	• powerful • extroverted • dominating • faithful • careful
low and sunken	• weak • introverted • submissive • inconsistent • careless

CHIN OR *DI GE*

The profile of the *di ge* or chin depicts the luck from 61 to 71. Firm, strong and square, and slightly protruding chins are better than weak, pointed and receding chins. Foreshortened chins depict an emotional personality. Strong and expressive chins portray firmness and perseverance. Double chins reflect inactivity in sports and games, as well as complacency in life. The cleft chin signifies compassion and sentiment. Many sports men have cleft chins, for example, American tennis player, Jimmy Connors. Chart 11 (page 100) summarises the different chins and their significance.

American tennis player Jimmy Connors.

Cheek bones too wide and chin square

Protruding chin

Strong chin

Set-back chin

Chart 11. Shapes of Chins and Their Significance

Chin	Significance
square and protruding slightly	• brave • enterprising • reliable • forthright (also, healthy stomach)
round and protruding slightly	• compassionate • humble • competent • tender (also, healthy stomach)
pointed and protruding slightly	• disciplined • imaginative • understanding • trusting (also, healthy stomach)
square and receding	• outgoing • open-minded • optimistic • complacent (also, strong heart)
round and receding	• pretentious • sociable • suspicious • apprehensive (also, strong heart)
pointed and receding	• carefree • pessimistic • shy • undisciplined (also, strong heart)

Moles and Wrinkles

MOLES

Moles are caused by pigment cells. There are a few types of moles—some are flat, some are fleshy, some have hairs. Some are black, some are brown, and some are very light in colour. Some moles are birth marks while others develop during childhood or adulthood. To the face reader, moles are significant indications of luck, good or bad. Figures 11 and 12 illustrate favourable and unfavourable moles on males and females.

One of China's greatest revolutionaries and strategists, former chairman Mao Ze Dong had a wang face and good facial features such as high cheek bones, broad forehead and a good mole.

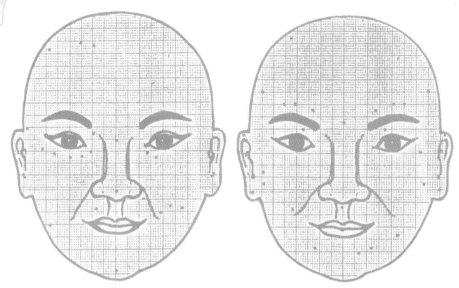

Figure 11. Bad (left) and good (right) luck moles for males

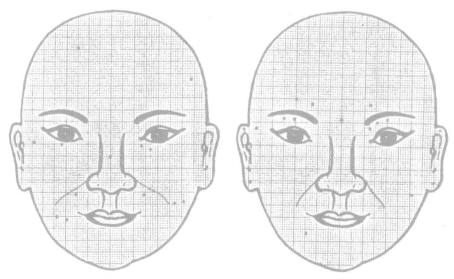

Figure 12. Bad (left) and good (right) luck moles for females.

WRINKLES

Wrinkles that indicate good luck are on the forehead in three parallel lines and they are even better if a vertical one crosses them. They should be firm and continuous. Broken wrinkles or lines are not as good. If there is only one single wrinkle across the forehead, it signifies poor luck during the later part of life. Figure 13 (page 104) shows both bad and good luck wrinkles.

Significant wrinkles on the *yin tang* signify power and longevity. When wrinkles appear on the *yin tang* and *zhong zheng* they can be good signs especially when they form the word *wang* 王 or three parallel lines. Some world leaders have these lines. George Cloony also has these lines.

Some people like to comb their hair over their foreheads to cover or hide wrinkles. My advice is not to since the forehead shows one's fortune, virtue, career and parental care. It is better to show this part of the face even at the expense of aesthetics. The sketch below shows that when the hair is combed over the forehead, the face may look imbalanced.

When hair is combed over the forehead, it can sometimes cause the face to look imbalanced.

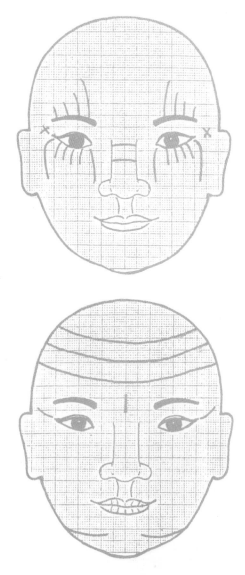

Figure 13. Bad (top) and good (bottom) luck wrinkles

Other Aspects of Face Reading

Face reading is not just confined to reading facial features. The face must be assessed with the individual's *qi* 气 (energy), *shen* 神 (spirit), *gu* 骨 (bone) and *sheng yin* 声音 (voice) in mind. For instance, good facial features do not guarantee longevity if the person's *qi, shen, gu* and *shen yin* are lacking in quality.

SHEN AND QI

Shen is the spirit hidden behind the physical facial features. It can be detected by looking at the colour of the face and the spirit of the eyes. Spirited eyes (ie, bright, shining eyes) indicate vigorous *shen* while dull eyes reveal a dissipated and exhausted *shen*. *Qi* is the energy of the body expressed by the colour and texture of the face.

It is difficult to separate *shen* and *qi*. Together *shen qi* is expressed on the face through its colour and texture. Smooth texture of the face reveals adequate *shen qi* in the person whereas rough and blemished texture indicates poor *shen qi*.

The colour of *shen qi* that is shown on the face informs the face reader about the wellbeing and fortune of the person. There are five colours on a person's face, namely, green, black, white, red and yellow. Chart 12 (page 106) shows the significance of the colour of *shen qi*.

There are 12 areas of the face, known as *gong*, that indicate particular relationships between the person and those around him, or a particular aspect of life (see Figure 14).

Chart 12. Colour of Shen Qi and its Significance

Colour	Significance
greenish and whitish	worries (but indicates luck if it appears on certain areas. See Chart 14 on page 109.)
blackish	illnesses
reddish	argument (may also indicate luck. See Chart 13 on page 108)
yellowish	auspiciousness

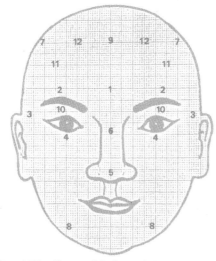

Figure 14. The 12 areas of the face and what they indicate.

The relationships governed by these areas are:

1. Fate
2. Brotherly love
3. Marital bliss
4. Relationship with children
5. Wealth
6. Sickness and calamity
7. Housing and settlement
8. Employee/employer relationship
9. Political power
10. Property
11. Virtues
12. Relationship with parents

If these areas are favourable as described in the earlier chapters, then these particular relationships or aspects of life represented would generally be good. However, if spots or discolourations are found on these areas (showing poor *shen qi*) problems may be encountered.

Generally, the various areas on the face are also representative of the 12 lunar months in a year. Each area is associated with colours. Refer to Figure 15 (page 108) to find out the area of face associated with the lunar month. Chart 13 maps out the favourable or unfavourable colours in relation to the lunar month.

Generally, certain colours signify poor health for certain areas, as shown in the Charts 13 and 14 on pages 108 and 109.

Grey and greenish colours depict misfortune especially when they occur on the *shan gen* (area of nose between eyes) or around the eyes. A yellowish colour indicates possible ill health but if it occurs on the *zhun tou* (tip of nose) up to the *yin tang* (on the nose) it depicts progress and luck. Pinkish colour on the cheeks depicts luck and romance. Although reddish colours are generally good, if they occur in a concentrated area or in a deep line on the nose or *shan gen*, they depict danger.

The colour of the eyebrows should be even. This means that the hair of the eyebrows should have the same intensity of colour throughout. Colour of the *yin tang* should not be greyish or marred by discolourations or the person could encounter calamities or setbacks in life. If red spots occur on the *yin tang* the person may encounter disputes that end in the court house.

Generally the colour of the face plays an important part in the indication of the person's health and mental state. It should generally be of even colour (although there are preferred colours, see sketches below). The face should not have patches of discolouration or marks or spots.

The leftmost face is of a favourable colour, while the rest are less favourable.

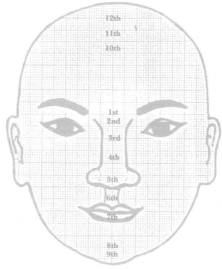

Figure 15. The 12 areas of face that represent the 12 lunar months.

Chart 13. Favourable and Unfavourable Colours in Relation to Lunar Month

Lunar Month	Favourable Colour	Unfavourable Colour
1st	greenish or reddish	white or yellowish
2nd	natural colour of skin	white or greenish
3rd	reddish	white or greenish
4th	reddish	white or greenish
5th	yellowish or reddish	greyish
6th	natural colour of skin	greenish
7th	natural colour of skin	greenish
8th	yellowish	grey
9th	natural colour of skin	reddish
10th	natural colour of skin	reddish
11th	natural colour of skin	dark grey
12th	natural colour of skin	dark grey

Chart 14. Areas of the Face and Corresponding Colours Showing Poor Luck and Health

Area	Colours Showing Poor Luck And Health
forehead	• grey • green • reddish (heart ailment)
yin tang (area between eyebrows)	• green (lung ailment) • red • white • grey (heart ailment)
shan gen (area of nose between eyes)	• grey • green (liver ailment)
nose	• green (liver ailment) • red (spleen ailment)
area above eyebrows	• white (lung ailment)
area surrounding eyes	• grey • green (lung or spleen ailment)
cheeks	• grey or red (kidney ailment)
ears	• grey (kidney ailment)
mouth	• green, grey or too red (heart ailment)
di ge (chin)	• grey • green (stomach ailment)

Gu (Bone)

How does one assess the bone structure in face reading? Ancient writings have the following to say:

- The bone structure should be well covered by the flesh. If the bones show, the person is not outstanding.
- The important bone profiles on the face are the forehead, eyebrow and cheeks.
- The amount of the flesh on the bones must be balanced. For example, if the person is thin the flesh covering the bone structure of the face should not be too thick.

Sheng Yin (Voice)

How is sound assessed? Ma Yin, a famous face reading master, said the following:

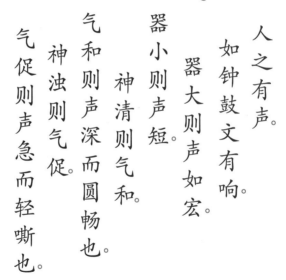

人之有声。
如钟鼓文有响。
器大则声如宏。
器小则声短。
神清则气和。
气和则声深而圆畅也。
神浊则气促。
气促则声急而轻嘶也。

In face reading, the sound that comes out of the mouth should come from the *dan tian* (below the navel) and the speech should be clearly made.

Translated, this means that a person has a voice just like a bell or drum making sounds. Big vessels make loud sounds and small vessels, short sounds. A pure spirit has harmonious *qi* (energy), which produces deep and smooth sounds. Impure spirits have impatient *qi,* which produces interrupted sounds.

PLASTIC SURGERY

What is it that makes a face look beautiful? What are the differences between very attractive and beautiful faces and less appealing faces? The Chinese have a saying: "*ge hua le ge yan*" (every flower has its own admirer, or in other words, one man's meat may be another's poison). So does plastic surgery changes one's face? Of course, it does. But does it change one's fortune or destiny? The answer is yes and no. Yes, because it does make one look like what one desires provided the surgery is most successful. But if it is not, then, obviously it will not be satisfactory. Try to imagine this: A man has an ordinary face with fleshy nose, high forehead and thick lips. He undergoes plastic surgery and has his fleshy nose changed to a thin tiny nose. He has his high forehead changed to a low forehead by having a hair implant. He then has his thick lips changed to thin lips. But his luck does not improve because his fleshy nose that depicts fortune has been changed to a thin tiny nose. This signifies poor fortune from the age of 41 to 50. His thick lips that once portrayed his compassion for others and his good fortune during the age of 60 has been altered to thin tight lips that depict meanness and heartlessness. He inadvertently lost his fortune becaused he changed his features. But another person with some knowledge of face reading and has his face changed from bad to good. However, his face features may change due to aging. In any case, since such features are man-made they may not depict the inner nature and talent of the person.

Can one change one's face without surgery? The answer is yes, although limited because when one changes one's personality one may change one's facial expressions. For example, if someone is always worrying over everything he/she might frown often. By so doing he/she forms lines on his/her forehead and wrinkles on his/her face. His/her *fa ling* are likely to be deep and reflect sadness and worry. Should he/she overcome his/her pessimistic outlook and take things much easier, over time his/her face might always look cheerful and portrays a different personality and different face.

Some Famous Faces Read

The earlier chapters show how a person's personality traits and his fortune are indicated in particular areas of his face. Facial features such as the forehead, the eyebrows, the eyes, the nose, the ears, the mouth, the cheeks and chin, not only reflect the inner self, but also reveal the fortune, good or bad, of a person. The good face is not just a pretty or handsome face. The facial features must be good in accordance with the theory of face reading.

Numerous real life examples have been given to help one get to know people better by reading their faces. More examples are given in the following pages, in the form of famous people through the ages from 551 BC to current times. Their facial features are analysed with reference to the milestones in their lives, to their successes and failures.

Years of age referred to in this section are calculated according to the Western calendar. For example, Confucius, who was born in the year 551 BC, was one year old in 550 BC and not two years old.

CONFUCIUS 孔夫子 (551–479 BC)

Nationality : Chinese
Occupation : Philosopher, Teacher, Writer

He was a thinker and social philosopher. His philosophy emphasized personal and public morality, social relationship, justice and sincerity. His teachings in the Analects were compiled after his death. In the Analects, Confucius emphasised the rule of behavior. Self-cultivation, emulation of moral exemplars and the attainment of skilled judgment became the ethics of his teachings.

Confucius was born into a poor but noble family. At 53 he rose to the position of Justice Minister in Lu. Soon after, the Duke neglected to send to Confucius a portion of the sacrificial meat that was his due according to custom, and Confucius seized this pretext to leave both his post and the state of Lu. He resigned to take a long journey around the small kingdoms of northeast and central China. Saddened by the loss of both his son and his favourite disciples he died at the age of 72.

Milestones in Life

Confucius was a self-made man. He lost his father at the age of 3. At 15, he worked as a clerk in the Memorial temple of the Duke of Zhou. At 21, he was one of the Secretaries of Justice at the imperial court. After his resignation he traveled widely. At 67 he retired in Lu. For five years he edited the famous *Wu Jing*, the *Five Canons of Confucius* (including *the Book of Changes, the Book of History, the Book of Poetry, the Book of Rites* and *the Book of Spring and Autumn*). He died at 72.

Analysis of Facial Features

From Confucius' face, the qualities of good human nature such as humility, love, magnanimity, honesty, determination and generosity can be detected. Although his childhood was not a period of material enjoyment, he was much inspired by his mother spiritually. His forehead and ears revealed such spiritual encouragement, and his personal achievement at 21. Although his life from 40 to 67 was not a period of idleness and enjoyment, his travels enriched his knowledge and wisdom. These were depicted by his nose, mouth and lips. His achievements from 67 to his death were just as great. He wrote and edited the *Wu Jing* which earned him recognition as a theorist and teacher.

GAIUS JULIUS CAESAR (100–44 BC)

Nationality : Roman
Occupation : Politician, General, Statesman

Julius Caesar formed an unofficial triumvirate with Marcus Crassus and Gnaeus Maggus, which dominated Roman politics for many years. His conquests enlarged the Roman world. Unfortunately, the triumvirate collapsed. So did his relationship with the senate. He then started a civil war in 49 BC and gained control of the government. He was proclaimed the dictator for life. Most unfortunately, a group of senators, led by Marcus Brutus killed him in 44 BC.

Milestones in Life

Born in 100 BC of noble family. His father died when he was 16. He was brought up by his dedicated mother. At 22, he became a prosecuting advocate. At 31, he was promoted but his wife died. At 37, he was made *pontifex maximus* (supreme pontiff of the highest religious authority).

As general, he won many victories, including the conquest of Gaul. At 51, in a civil war, he drove his political opponents out of Italy. He later proclaimed himself dictator.

Although he was very physically strong, his life was put to an end when he was brutally murdered at the age of 56.

Analysis of Facial Features

Caesar's facial features indicates that he was brilliant (his eyes were large and intelligent). He was hard (his lips were not balanced, with thin upper lip and thick lower lip, and his nose was not really straight). He was also very determined; he had firm lips and bushy eyebrows. His forehead and ears reflect his good upbringing and powerful family background. He had a powerful nose and won many victories from the age of 40 onwards. His left *fa ling* and hollow cheeks indicated his violent death at 56.

CAO CAO 曹操 (AD 155–220)

Nationality : Chinese
Occupation : Politician

During the Three Kingdom era, Cao Cao was a regional warlord, the chancellor of the Eastern Han Dynasty. Some historical records portray him as a cruel tyrant, while some regard him as a brilliant military leader. At 20, Cao Cao became a captain and was later sent from Luoyang to Yingchuan to deal with rebels. He was successful

and became a Governor. He raised his own army, and joined other warlords to fight against Dong Zhuo, a powerful warlord. When Cao Cao was 41 he became more powerful and influential as the General-in-chief and Marquis.

When Cao Cao was 58 he was bestowed the title, Duke of Wei, and had ten cities under his control. At 61 Cao Cao was proclaimed the King of Wei.

Milestones in Life

He was born in AD 155 into a family of wealth and power. At 20 he took office as attending officer of Emperor Han Xi. Later he was sent to Luoyang as an administrator. There was internal revolt and he was assigned the duty of military leader when he was 29. In AD 189, the Emperor passed away but his successor was only 14, so Dong Zhuo, the evil Rector of the imperial court, assumed power and appointed another emperor who was only nine years old. Cao Cao retired and left the capital. However, to regain power he sought the alliance of others and formed a military powerful enough to challenge Dong Zhuo. At 41, Cao Cao became a very powerful military leader. At 53, he became Prime Minister. He died at 66.

Analysis of Facial Features

Cao Cao had long and well-formed ears that depicted his powerful family background and good upbringing. His forehead was extensive and well-formed—at 20 he was offered a post by the emperor. His *yin tang* (area between eyebrows) was full and his eyebrows are quite far apart. Thus there was a change in his life, a turning point, which led him to hold military power later on. His nose represented power, luck and determination, thus, from 40 to 50, he became powerful, influential and successful. His weak features were his thin lips. He did not live beyond 66.

ZHUGE LIANG 诸葛亮 (AD 181–234)

Nationality : Chinese
Occupation : General, Political Adviser

During the Three Kingdom era, Zhuge Liang was Chancellor of Shu Han. He was and to some is the greatest and most accomplished strategist of his era.

Zhuge Liang was born in Shandong Province. His mother died when he was nine, and his father when he was 12. He was then raised by his uncle.

Zhuge Liang joined one of the warlords, Liu Bei, in 207 and became Liu's strategist. In 208, the allied armies of Liu Bei and another warlord, Sun Quan, defeated Cao Cao. Zhuge Liang became the Regent and he aimed to restore the Han Dynasty. From 228 till his death in 234, Zhuge Liang launched five Northern Expeditions. On the fifth expedition, he died of illness at the age of 53.

Milestones in Life

He lived a life of a recluse until he was 27. Internal war broke out when he was three year-old. When he was 27, a feudal lord, Liu Bei, went personally three times to his hut to urge him to become his political adviser. He agreed and by the age 40 he became Prime Minister to Liu Bei. He led a highly successful and accomplished life. He died at 53.

Analysis of Facial Features

Zhu's forehead was ordinary and his eyebrows were rather short, thus his life during his younger days, from 3 to 17, was a hard life full of turmoil and disappointment. But his eyes were well-formed and he reached the peak of his career by the age of 40, when he became Prime Minister. He was intelligent and resourceful, but he lived a short life as his *ren zhong* was rather short.

EMPRESS WU ZETIAN 武则天 (AD 624–705)

Nationality : Chinese
Occupation : Empress during the Tang dynasty

Wu Zetian was the only woman in the history of China to assume the title of Empress Regnant. When she founded the Zhou dynasty in 690, she held on to her power and attended to all political affairs personally.

At the age of 13, Zetian entered the palace and became a concubine of Emperor Tai Zong who passed away in 649. She was supposed to spend the rest of her life in a nunnery. However, through an unlikely fortuity—Empress Wang, wife of Emperor Gaozong, son of Tai Zong, wanted another beauty to challenge Gao Zong's favourite concubine, consort Xiao—Zetian was brought back to the palace. She was fated to became the Empress when Gao Zong, made her his Empress when his first wife was killed. She gained more and more power. Towards the end of Emperor Gao Zong's reign, she became the empress dowager. To seize full control of the throne, she deposed her son, Zhong Zong, and had her youngest son, Rui Zong, made emperor. In 690, she had Emperor Rui Zong abdicated and established the Zhou Dynasty.

Milestones in Life

Wu Zetian was born in 624 into a powerful family. Her father was a government official and her mother was the daughter of a former prime minister of the Sui dynasty which preceded the Tang dynasty. When she was 11, her father died and she and her mother were ill-treated by her father's first wife. At 14, she was brought into the imperial household as a concubine of Tang Tai Zong. She did not become a favourite of Tai Zong's. So she was lonely from the ages of 14 to 26 although she was living in the palace. When she was 25, the emperor died and she was sent to a nunnery. At 28, she was readmitted to the palace as a concubine of the emperor Tang Gao Zong. At 42, she became empress and ruled the country until her death at 80.

Analysis of Facial Features

Empress Wu's forehead and temple were full and broad indicating that she was born into a wealthy and powerful family. Her left ear may have had a defect as her father died when she was 11. Her luck changed when she turned 28 (her *zheng zhong* [lower forehead] and *yin tang* [area between the eyes] were well-formed). Her eyebrows were well-shaped and her nose, straight and prominent. Thus her life from 28 to 50 was successful. Indeed her crowning moment came when she was 42 when she rose to the throne (notice her powerful cheeks). Her *ren zhong* (depression above the lips), which was very long, indicated her long and powerful life.

YUE FEI 岳飞 (1103–1142)

Nationality : Chinese
Occupation : Military General

There are many stories about Yue Fei, one relates how he purchased a bow and spear to learn the art of archery at an early age. He practiced martial art diligently and became a master of 18 types of weapons.

Another story tells of a monk came and warned Yue Fei's father to put his wife and newborn child inside a water tank if the baby were to cry. Three days later, the baby cried loudly, so Yue's father put his family in a boat on the yellow river. Yue's father drowned; his mother raised him by doing needle work.

Milestones in Life

By the age of 28, he was a patriotic warrior serving the Song emperor, Song Gao Zhong. He won numerous battles, but in 1141, at the age of 38, traitors plotted against him so that he would fall out of favour with the emperor. The following year, he was framed by his enemies and executed.

Analysis of Facial Features

His forehead was broad and full; and he had the support and love of his mother and family. Before he joined the army, his mother tattooed four characters on his back: *jin zhong bao guo* 尽忠报国 which means, complete loyalty to the country. His heroic and courageous nature was shown in his broad forehead and slightly slanting eyebrows (*jian mei*). His eyes were too slanted (upward) and not well-delineated. It was not surprising that his luck was bad at the age of 39 when his treacherous enemies killed him.

BEN JONSON (1573–1637)

Nationality : English
Occupation : Poet, Dramatist and Novelist

Ben Johnson was one of the leading poets and literary scholars of his day. He was multi-talented—a well-known playwright, poet, writer and critic. His father died before he was born. He joined the army to avoid following his stepfather's trade as a brick layer. He became a theatrical writer after his army days.

Ben's misfortune came in 1597 when he was briefly imprisoned for writing a seditious play. He was known to have a hot temper and was tried at the Old Bailey on a charge of murder. He was found guilty but was subsequently set free.

Ben's fortunes changed when he was recognised for his poetry and works in 1616.

Milestones in Life

He was born in 1573, a few months after his father's death. Although he was sent to a private school, he left at 15 to work as a bricklayer. He married at about 21. By 25 he was acknowledged for his works but he allegedly killed an actor in a duel and was imprisoned. At 33, he became more well-known for his works. This was the turning point of his life. Through intervention of his friends, he was released from prison. His success was sustained until he was 53. At 55, he suffered from a stroke. He retired, and eventually died at the age of 64.

Analysis of Facial Features

Jonson's face revealed the hardship he experienced during his youth. His eyes and *ba zhi mei* (eyebrows) depicted frustration and sadness. His nose was well-formed except that its *shan gen* (part of nose between the eyes) showed the sign of violence. His forehead with wide temples showed that he was a great artist and poet. His *zheng zhong* (lower forehead) was full and so at 25 he began to be known for his works. But his success was marred when he was accused of murder. His eyebrows sloped down from the *zheng zhong* and this was not a good sign. However, his luck changed at 33 and his good and productive period was reflected in his strong and fleshy straight nose. His lips were well-formed so although he suffered from a few strokes, he survived them and lived to 64.

CHARLES SUMNER (1811–1874)

Nationality : American
Occupation : Politician

Charles was known for his stand against slavery. He was born in Boston and graduated from Harvard University. In 1851, he was elected to the United States Senate. A member of the Senate until his death, Sumner waged an uncompromising battle against slavery. He delivered some significant speeches on the Senate floor on slavery.

He was chairman of the Senate Committee on Foreign Relations from 1861 to 1871. He died in Washington, D.C. on March 11, 1874.

Milestones in Life

Charles Sumner graduated from Harvard Law School when he was 23. He left America for Europe when he was 26 and returned to the United States when he was 29. He lectured at Harvard and became a senator at the age of 41. He was successful in his career, but his marriage broke down when he was 55. He died at the age of 63.

Analysis of Facial Features

His prominent forehead revealed that his youth was blessed with success and recognition. Thus he graduated from one of the best universities in the United States. His eyes were very close to his nose thus he was away from home at the age of 26 and 27. His lower temples (shan lin) were well-defined and formed, signifying his return and obtaining a job at Harvard. His nose was straight, well-formed and prominent and he became famous and remained successful until well over 50.

SUN YAT-SEN 孙中山 (1866–1925)

Nationality : Chinese
Occupation : First President of the Chinese Republic

Sun Yatsen was and is still widely respected and revered by people the Chinese. He was well-loved as a revolutionary and political leader during his time. He played an important role in the eventual fall of the Qing Dynasty in 1911. He founded the Republic of China and then the Guomingdang (Nationalists). But his presidency did not last. His followers split into two parties after his death, but he left behind his political philosophy on nationalism, democracy and socialism.

Milestones in Life

At the age of 13, he left for America to study. At 17, he went to Hong Kong to study medicine, graduating at 26. He practised medicine in Hong Kong but was very involved in politics. He allied himself with anti-Manchu groups (the Manchu ruled China under the Qing dynasty from 1644 to 1911) to achieve his political goals—to free China from the Manchus. At 45 he returned to China as a national hero and became the first president of the Chinese republic following the overthrow of the Qing dynasty by the Nationalists. Shortly after, he resigned in favour of Yuan Shi Kai. At 47, he attempted to revolt against Yuan but failed and fled to seek foreign aid. He reorganised the Guomingdang (Nationalists) in efforts to bring about national unity. He died at 60 without achieving it.

Analysis of Facial Features

The shape of Sun's face (elongated with extensive temples) and facial features reflect his kindness, patriotism and dynamic personality. His forehead, well-shaped, and his ears, large and well-formed, indicated his good upbringing and opportunity to be educated.

His *yin tang* (area between the eyebrows) and *ling yun* (areas above the eyebrows) were well-shaped, fully developed, thus he graduated with a medical degree and started to practise medicine at the age of 26. His aspirations, ambitions and drive were expressed in his eyes which were well-delineated. His nose was very well-shaped and delineated (neither pointed nor broad) and he was well-respected, very well-known and he achieved his goals from 40 to 45. He faced setbacks and disappointments at 47 and 48. The lower part of his face was not as good as the upper part. He did not have a very long life.

JOSEPH VISSARIONOVICH STALIN (1879–1953)

Nationality : Russian
Occupation : Politician

Joseph Stalin became general secretary of the Communist Party of the Soviet Union Central Committee from 1922 until his death in 1953. He made many significant changes during his powerful reign such as speeding up economic growth, launching industrialisation of factories, as well as the collectivisation of agriculture. He brought the Soviet Union into the limelight during the World War II by joining other countries to defeat Nazi Germany.

Milestones in Life

Stalin's father died when he was 11. At 15, he matriculated from school. By 19 he was under the influence of Marxism. At 22 he became a member of the Social Democratic

Committee (a communist group). He was imprisoned at 23 for his political activities. Stalin became prominent at 33 and was appointed Commissar of Nationalities. At 43, he became secretary general of the Communist party. At 50 he became premier of the Soviet Union. He died at the age of 74.

Analysis of Facial Features

From his forehead it is evident that he did not have an easy life at youth. His *tian ting* (mid forehead) was good so at the age of 19 his life changed for the better. But at the age of 23 he faced a setback for a year, as indicated by the left and right upper foreheads or *bian cheng* that were covered with hair. His strong, bushy and powerful eyebrows indicated that his luck would change at age 34. His prominent nose and eyes spelt leadership from 40 to 50 and showed his tenacity, intelligence and firmness. Even his square jaws and powerful chin revealed his drive and his ambition. He lived to a ripe old age of 74 as evidenced by his well-formed left cheek bone.

MAO ZEDONG 毛泽东 (1893–1976)

Nationality : Chinese
Occupation : Politician

Mao Zedong was and is still regarded by the Chinese as the most prominent political leader and revolutionist. The world recognises him as one of the most prominent figures in modern history.

Milestones in Life

Mao was born in 1893 into a prosperous family in a village in Hunan. At 25, he finished school and left home for Beijing. He returned in 1919 and founded the Chinese Communist Party in 1921. He consolidated his authority during the Long

March from 1934 to 1935. He became chairman of the party at the age of 38. He became very powerful and triumphed over the Nationalists in 1949, establishing the People's Republic of China, at the age of 56. By the age of 60 his influence grew throughout the Communist orbit. At 73 he retired as Party Chairman of the Chinese Communist Party but continued to be very influential and initiated the Cultural Revolution to recreate the revolutionary spirit. It only ended after his death in 1976, at the age of 83.

Analysis of Facial Features

The most striking features of Mao's face were his cheek bones, his forehead, his nose and his big mole on the *di ge* (chin). Mao's face was essentially *mu*-shaped although it was not very long. His face revealed that he was resourceful, determined and a born leader. He was able to take setbacks and bounce back with vigour. His forehead was wide, well-formed and smooth, reflecting that he was born into a fairly well-to-do family and that he was highly intelligent. His eyes showed vigilance and persuasive powers. They also revealed wisdom and intelligence. His powerful and straight nose indicated success and capability from the age of 41 to 50. His prominent *quan* affirmed his ability to command obedience and respect from his subordinates. The line of his lips were firm and curved slightly upwards indicating that his influence would spread beyond his homeland. His *fa ling* and strong chin confirmed that he had a good life after 50. His famous mole (below the lips) was a lucky mole.

FURTHER READING

Eacker, Jay, *Problems of Metaphysics and Psychology*, Nelson Hall, Chicago, 1983.
Needham, Joseph, *Science and Civilization on China*, London, 1982.
Schiffman, Harvey Richard, *Sensation and Perception*, John Wiley and Sons, 1976.

SELECTED BOOKS AND ARTICLES BY EVELYN LIP
Lip, Evelyn, *Chinese Geomancy*, Times Books International, Singapore, 1979.
Lip, Evelyn, *Chinese Beliefs and Superstitions*, Graham Brash, Singapore, 1985.
Lip, Evelyn, *Notes on Things Chinese*, Graham Brash, 1988.